Y0-BRZ-406

To Anne - thanks for your help. — mike

THE
RE-CREATION
OF A NATION

Through Real Parenting

by

MICHAEL J. MAYER

Michael J. Mayer

R & E Publishers ❖ Saratoga, CA

R & E Publishers
P.O. Box 2008, Saratoga, CA 95070
Tel: (408) 866-6303   Fax: (408) 866-0825

Book Design and Typesetting by Diane Parker
Cover by Kaye Quinn

Library of Congress Card Catalog Number: **92-54174**

ISBN 0-88247-929-6

CONTENTS

1

WHY MUST I READ A BOOK ON PARENTING?

"Look, another book on telling us how to be a good parent; <u>Ten Easy Steps to an Enjoyable Life with Your Children</u>. I don't need this book. Our kids are just fine. They come home at night. They enjoy life. In fact, I hardly know they are around. Now this book might be good for my neighbors and their kids. You should see them. . . ."

"What else could be new in parenting? I have read all the books and still nothing helps me with my child. I set limits and I love them. I am afraid of what they are going to tell me next."

"He doesn't know my kid. How can he know the pain and agony I go through in trying to raise my child? They all think they know the answers and then they tell me in words that don't mean anything to me."

And on and on and on go the doubts and concerns of parents. Parents who have tried so very hard to raise their children properly; parents who haven't tried hard but are still reaching out for answers in their lives and the lives of their children. These parents and more continue to search for answers, for help, for relief, and most importantly for joy in being a parent. As I sit here writing this book, I get chills up and down my spine. Chills because I want to be able to explain to you what I have seen happening with families in my 16 years of experience as a psychologist. Chills because the answer is so simple that it will not be recognized. So difficult because it is so easy to hear but it is often disregarded. So exciting because it is in reach of many families. I am afraid of the challenge, as it is so difficult to write something that those reading the words will interpret in a way that is meaningful to their families and to themselves.

The style I have decided to use in conveying the message to you about being an effective parent will come in words from my emotional, spiritual, physical, and intellectual parts that joined together to make me. I will not let the technical words interfere with my presentation to you. It will only confuse you. Therefore, you are in for a treat. I hope to be able to touch a chord in you that will bring about a change in your responding to self, life, *and family*. As you read this book, you will notice that at times I will use the pronoun "he" and sometimes I will use the pronoun "she." The pronoun "he" or the pronoun "she" will be used to denote both sexes.

In order to be able to learn from what I write, you will need to do something that will be a positive change in your life. Open your mind to new meanings to words, to new concepts, to new ways of interpreting what you have already learned. You are probably saying, "I can do that." Yes, you can until I hit an area that is sensitive to you. Then your defense system goes into play and interprets what you read or learn into your own words that are more acceptable, or else you reject it entirely. To get around these blocks you will need to keep reminding yourself to keep your interpretation open for the time being. If you do this *you will learn so much*!! You will continue to be your own teacher, your own source of knowledge. I will remind you to keep your mind open as I write.

Several thoughts may help you convince your mind that it should allow new thoughts into its storage tank.

Wisdom is admitting that you know nothing. The more you know, the more you realize what you do not know.

Change is continual. You are constantly in the process of change. Some change will occur with our permission; other change will occur without our permission. You often fight change, but it will occur, despite your best intentions.

You form definitions for words the day you start speaking. "Mama" and "dada" take on meaning to the very young child. Words take on meaning to the very young child. Words take on definitions that you formulate through your experiences. That meaning of the word is your meaning. The meaning of these words as so stated by Leo Buscaglia will either "cage you or free you."[1] Your meanings to words can send you into your own "hell" or your own "heaven" on earth. Your meanings to words and your responses to those meanings could lead to depression, compulsions, panic, phobias, or to happiness, contentment, personal affirmation. I sincerely hope that you allow the words I write to "free" you and help you grow into that positive being you wish to be.

Several quotes from a book by Father Leo Booth[2] illustrate the point I am trying to make:

"The foolish and the dead never change their opinions."   JAMES RUSSELL LOWELL

"Not ignorance, but ignorance of ignorance is the death of knowledge."   ALFRED NORTH WHITEHEAD

"Nothing will ever be attempted if all possible objections must be first overcome."   SAMUEL JOHNSON

"The brighter you are, the more you have to learn."
                                                    DON HEROLD

"Sixty years ago I knew everything; now, I know nothing; education is a progressive discovery of our own ignorance."   WILL DURANT

I continue my efforts with you to be aware of your potential to read the words in this book and learn so much or nothing. That will be your choice.

Gaining new knowledge is not easy. We often forget what we learned or we distort what we learn to fit what we already know. What a shame! I wish I didn't do that. I learn so much more when I am not defensive or being bull-headed in being right.

I want you to feel that I am with you as you read my words. I want you to be personally involved in the book. I will tend to use fewer words than most people would expect. This is because I value your time as precious.

My goal in writing this book is to help you alter your thinking and feeling enough to bring about the change you need to deal more effectively with self and life in relation to your children. A rewarding experience, indeed!

In future chapters as we focus on the individual within the family, it is important to be aware that I consider the individual to be composed of four parts: spiritual, emotional, intellectual, and physical. I feel the individual needs to be healthy in each of the four areas. Religious leaders offer many the guidance needed to express their spirituality. Medical doctors and related professionals offer help to many with their physical concerns. Teachers provide the help to many in the start of their education. Mental Health professionals are offering help to many in their quest for emotional health. There is someone for every aspect of man's being. Good professionals work together to help others and themselves integrate their life. In dealing with your children, you need to be aware of their progression in each of these areas. A deficit in any one area could put the child/adolescent into "tilt" or off-balance. A self-examination may be in order to judge how *you* fare in these four components of your life.

As humans we all want the same thing: To love and be loved. We often "botch" this up. This seems so simple but it is the greatest of all the achievements of human beings and takes more fortitude and courage than any other *feat*. We learn what love means as a child and carry this meaning into adulthood, into marriage and into our children and their children. If our love is lacking, we pass that along also. We need a definition of love that "frees us not cages us."

THOUGHTS

- Keep an open mind and you will learn.

- Parenting is so difficult, yet so positively simple.

- We all have a lot to learn about parenting.

- We all have a lot to learn about loving.

- To change is to be alive.

1   Buscaglia, Leo, Loving, Living, Learning, 1982, Holt, Rinehart, Winston, NY, p. 45.

2   Booth, Leo, Say Yes to Life, Health Communications, Inc., Pompano Beach, FL.

2 WHERE DO I START?

Parenting is one of the most important aspects of human existence and at the same time a very challenging task. As parents we are trying to help a new life develop into a total human being. We have the power to shape the future for our child. This process affects our child's growth and development and will carry on into generations. How we handle our children will affect other children yet to be born. Being a parent is the only way any human being is guaranteed of influencing another person's life. No power is greater than that of a parent. Children, no matter how treated, will always be influenced by their biological parents. Once a child is born, the parents cannot hand their power over to anyone else. The influence belongs to them for the rest of that child's life.

Parenting is not an easy task. We need to remain open-minded to new ideas and not be afraid to challenge our present beliefs.

Starting to learn new concepts, adjust old ones, throw some out, and momentarily give up in disgust seems to be in order. Order? What is in order being a parent? Not much, but there may be some help to gain *some* order to the chaos that sometimes or often times happens in a typical household.

Where should the focus be in learning to parent? Generally, it is in learning how to take what you already know and readjust it to make it work more effectively. Also adding a little more knowledge through other's parenting experiences could help. Parents need to know how to love, and discipline or set limits. Setting limits includes a discussion on spanking, use of time out, use of positive rewards, and logical consequences. Creative use of your own skills in parenting can be developed. Inherited characteristics of your child need to be in your awareness as you begin to notice differences in behavior from one child to the next.

Other concerns to be mentioned in your quest to be a better parent include awareness of the expectations you place on your child, the messages you send your child, and a discussion of the effects of divorce on your children.

Isn't that enough? No! The key is still missing, yet not missing, as it will be discussed throughout the book. What can be so important? Read on. Somewhere, somehow, by some power greater than I, *you can let* the most important key to effective parenting touch an inner chord of real recognition. It will have to touch you from the top of your head to the bottom of your toes, through and through. Anything less will only decrease its importance. Yes, it is the key, but you must let it find you, find your heart, soul, spirit, mind, and body. Let it reach you. If you keep it, your life will change dramatically in a positive direction. To lose sight of it will only put you back until you regain it again. The key lies within you but it is mentioned in this book. I hope that each reader finds it and uses it. I haven't decided if I will let you find the key or tell you my perception of the *key*. I do know one thing. My experiences with children, adolescents, and adults for sixteen intense years tells me that I am right about this being the key to being an effective parent.

With the proper attitude, you will find the key within this book. Read on.

THOUGHTS

- Parenting influences everyone.

- Parenting has implications that reach the soul of a child and the heart of a nation.

- There is a *key* to parenting and it is within your power to find it.

- Be open to finding this key.

- Ask yourself, what do you think is the key to parenting?

3 THE FIRST ABILITY: TO LOVE

To be an effective parent, believe it or not, you only need two abilities: love and effective limit setting. As you read those words, I am sure the thought went through your mind, "I love my children and I know how to discipline them." If that were true, if everyone knew how to effectively love and discipline their children, we would not see the problems that are arising today with our children.

The word love has as many meanings as there are people reading this book. Let me tell you some of the meanings I have encountered in working with families and children. Love to some children means a hug, kiss, or the statement, "I love you." To other children it might be a touch or a kind word. Sometimes love means simply spending time with a child. Some children have told me that their parents find it hard to be affectionate and loving toward them; the only way their parents can express love to them is by spending time with them. A few children have said their parents show them love by providing for them—providing food, clothing, and a home. To a few kids, a beating was the only form of love they knew.

Love can be a combination of many forms of behavior, words, and expressions. Love is typically shown through hugs, touches, kisses, "I love you's;" but no matter how love is shown, it must be shown to the child consistently. Children typically like to be hugged and told they are loved. Many children, however, grow up not having experienced these hugs and kisses and "I love you's." Consequently, they look for other expressions of caring from their parents. As mentioned earlier, these other expressions of caring might be a simple pat on the back or buying something for the child when he does something good. That form of love we show our children when growing up will greatly influence the form of love that our children, when adults, will seek from others, especially a spouse. Let me give you an example.

John is now seven years old and lives in a family where neither the mother nor the father are capable of outwardly expressing affection. As John grows up, he learns that his parents care for him because they constantly work to provide nice things for him. Mother works so that the extras can be bought. John is also aware that his parents treat him fairly. They do not demand too much of him nor are they unfair in their punishment when he does something wrong. Love to John means being cared for and provided for. John probably does not expect physical nor verbal expressions of love. When John grows up and decides to marry, he probably will express his love toward the woman he chooses to marry in the form of providing for her and taking care of her well-being. He probably will not be affectionate toward her. It will be much easier for him to provide for her than to express his caring.

As parents, we choose to show love to our children. The methods and the style of love shown is entirely our choice. Our methods of loving our children have been greatly influenced by the methods that we learned earlier in our lives. People who touch encourage touching within the family; and people who hug develop hugging within their families. Family members imitate the expressions of love they show one another.

You will find me trying to encourage parents to show love to their children. *All the discipline methods that you want to use with your children will be ineffective if you do not show your child love.* A child who is not shown love will find it difficult to obey. *Love is the basis, for a child's wanting to obey, to respect the feelings and rights of others.*

Most of us are very poor at consistently showing love to our children. We forget to praise our children. We often forget to take time to tell them we are glad they are our son or daughter. I often ask parents to be sure to give each child and adult in the family some positive expression of caring at least once a day.

Believe me, without the feeling of being loved, it is very hard to convince anyone to do anything. If you have not learned to express your love to your children, maybe you need to work on that problem before you begin to try a lot of discipline techniques with them.

Ask yourself of the following questions and put the answers on a sheet of paper so you can review them from time to time.

QUESTION 1:   When you were a child, how did your mother show you she loved you? What forms of love did your mother display toward you? Was it a hug, a kiss, praise, spending time with you, a combination of these things, or a completely different form of expression?

QUESTION 2:   Answer the same questions with regard to your father.

QUESTION 3:   How did your mother discipline you? What methods did your mother use to get you to obey? For example, did she use spanking, the belt, making you stand in the corner, taking away your privileges, or another choice?

QUESTION 4:   Answer those questions with regard to your father.

QUESTION 5:   How do you show love to your children today?

QUESTION 6:   How do you discipline your children today?

The answers to these questions will help you compare the methods that you use in showing love and discipline toward your children with those you learned from your parents. Some of you changed methods because you vowed never to use those your parents used. But if you look more closely, you will find that you have picked up more traits of your parents than originally thought. What you might see is that the underlying principles are similar although the forms used may vary somewhat.

Be aware that the methods used with your children might be similar to your parents' methods so that when you choose to change these methods you are at least cognizant of their origins. It is very hard to change these styles and ways of doing things. Being attuned to why you do things often makes it easier to change those methods.

You may need to find ways to show more love and caring for your children. Let me give you some suggestions that you may or may not already practice. Add your own methods of showing love to the list below.

1. *Hug your children at least once a day.* Hugs are healthy. Human beings need to be hugged.

2. *Kiss your children.* We never outgrow our need to be kissed. As children grow older, they sometimes shy away from being kissed. Maybe kisses will not be needed as often as a child grows older, but do not be afraid to continue this form of expressing love. It is only a social custom that tells us we shouldn't kiss our children when they get older. A small percentage of people shy away from kissing older children for fear that kissing implies a sexual meaning. It is good to be able to teach our children that kissing does not have to be associated with sexuality.

3. *Tell your children that you love them.* Many parents find it very hard to say "I love you." I would never want a parent to say that they loved their children if they did not mean it. I am assuming that you do love your children and therefore, you are capable of saying "I

love you." If you don't love your child, you need to find out why.

4. *Touch your child.* The touch can be a pat on the back, a gently holding of the arm, an arm around the shoulder, or touching his or her hand with yours. Whatever form you choose, to touch is important. Here again, it is so important to convey to your children through example that touching does not have to have a sexual meaning. If we teach our children the idea that touching means caring, then they will be more likely to appreciate the proper attitude and respect for touch.

5. *Praise your child.* A little bit of encouragement can go a very long way. Words of kindness make the child feel good inside. Praise can take many forms. Several examples might be: "You did a good job." "You look especially nice today." "I am glad you are my son." "It is nice to see you happy." "I am proud of your good work." "You have such a pretty smile."

6. *Love your child from an inner feeling.* You need to feel acceptance and love for your child within yourself. Don't fake your love. If you are upset with your child at the moment, don't say that you love him as he might become very confused about the meaning of your love. Wait until your frustration lessens and then express your love with true meaning.

A love is so precious. Love is life. Your child will always be unhappy and searching if he does not feel love from you. Love does not mean giving children total freedom to do what they want. Love is not concerned with the issue of freedom; that issue falls under the category of discipline. Love is a feeling for someone, a feeling that makes a person grow as a human being. I have included here a letter from a young lady who wishes she could have received positive love from her parents. She is still suffering today from the lack of this love. She really didn't ask for much.

"Throughout the years of growing up, and continuing now, the negative responses given to me by my parents have played a tremendous role in how I feel about myself. Never hearing a positive thing helped to form my very low self-esteem. It became something I not only expected from my parents, but also people around me. Things like, 'You're so fat.' 'That dress looks awful.' 'So you got a B, it should have been an A.' 'I don't think you could do anything right.' 'You are really stupid.' 'You are so lazy.' 'You aren't bright enough to make a decision.' These became an everyday thing. My parents have *never* said anything positive to me! Even now at 40, I still find myself unable to do anything for fear of the negative response. It is as if I go into everything expecting the worst, expecting to be a failure. I really believe that I will never be able to do anything that will draw a positive response from my parents. It has left deep marks on my life. It is a case of emotional abuse that can destroy lives, and almost did destroy mine.

"I have worked very hard as a mother to try and give positive feedback to my children. My father tells us how he knows it all, and we know nothing. He says those things to us to give us corrective criticism. It sure corrected us all right, we were afraid to sneeze.

"Oh, wouldn't it have felt good to once hear, 'You are a good kid.' 'You sure look good today.' 'I know you are capable of making a decision, but if you have a problem I am here.' Just telling your child you are proud of him or her, might someday save his or her life."

It would really be wonderful if parents could love their children unconditionally. The word "unconditional" is what is so important. No matter what your children do, you will always accept them and care for them. You will always be there. At no time do you lose sight of the fact that your children need acceptance. You accept their being. *You accept them. No "ifs."*

In the next chapter, I will mention another aspect of showing love to your children. Remember as you read to let new concepts into your system.

Does this chapter you just finished contain the key? Examine how you feel about what you read in relation to your own children.

THOUGHTS

- Praise your child at least one time a day.

- Hug your child at least one time a day (with true feeling).

- Loving a child makes him more appreciative of himself and of life.

- Reach out to your most prized possessions, your children.

- To love and to be loved should be of the highest priority (after basic needs are met).

- Do you feel loved? Have you ever felt love? Are you capable and willing to share your love with others?

- You can't love someone you fear or be loved by someone who fears you.

4 ANOTHER VIEW OF LOVE

Love is such an elusive word. It has so many meanings to so many people. Yet in the name of love many positive and negative things happen in our lives. We fall in love. We fall out of love. We need love. We want love. Many, many books have been written with love as the theme. There is an aspect of love or caring that I feel needs a little more emphasis than has been given in the past. That emphasis has to do with what is necessary in a relationship between a parent and a child. This might be the most important and critical information that you obtain in reading this book.

Let us begin by saying that I have learned to work on the premise that all young adults and children need love and caring from their parents. I also believe that this love needs to be an unconditional love from their parents.

What do I mean by unconditional love? Unconditional love carries the meaning that despite all of the behaviors of your child there is still acceptance of him. *That acceptance needs to be expressed!!!* An acceptance that as a child, he knows that his parents don't approve of what he did, but they will never leave him as a parent. They will never leave him emotionally. They will never stop loving him. The unconditional love needs to continue no matter how frustrating the behavior of the child becomes. An example of what I mean would be the parent who has a young adult who abuses drugs and alcohol and continually comes home drunk. After having tried an appropriate amount of therapy, along with other options to correct this behavior, if the young adult still refuses to stop his abuse of drugs and alcohol, then the parents need to say, "You can no longer live in this house." Or a second option, if he has not been hospitalized, say, "You need treatment." Both of these choices would be very difficult and you would be removing the child from the home. You don't stop loving the child even though you may have told him that he needs to find a residence somewhere else until he is willing to accept the limits set for the household.

It is very hard to separate your feelings at that time—feelings of anger that the child, that the young adult will not do as he is told; feelings of hurt; feelings of frustration. These feelings may show temporarily. But the bottom line is that you still care for the child. You still love your child. That love will not disappear. He is your child. She is your child. *Forever*! They grow up! They do take on their own values, beliefs, and attitudes, but they still need to know that Mom and Dad love them! You may not approve, as parents, but you still love them. You may not approve of what your children are doing; the lifestyle they lead; the actions they take; but you still *love* them. I cannot emphasize that enough!

Below is a letter from a young lady to her mother. She is talking about a problem in the family that has been handed down in the family for generations. There is not the emotional acceptance between mother and daughter. There has been a distance between mother and daughter for years and this was true going back three generations. It seems that the oldest daughter was to be a parent in the family; act like a parent; be an adult; yet very little warmth or emotion was allowed to be expressed openly and/or accepted openly. This was not a conscious process on the parent's part or on the mother's part. The daughter, because of the approach used by the mother, did not feel accepted by her mother or by her father. It is so easy to trace the roots of the problem back to and through the mother's side of the family. There is a definite "rejection pattern", but the rejection was not a conscious process by anyone. The daughter picked up the rejection and had a very difficult time until she confronted it and expressed this confrontation in a letter. This is a sad example, of what can happen in a family without the family being the slightest bit aware of what is going on. When the mother was told this she stood back and said, "I don't believe it! I don't believe that I did that to my daughter." After some time of looking at how her daughter perceived her, the mother began to understand how she affected her child and immediately realized that she felt the very same way toward her mother, the daughter's grandmother.

Here is the letter of the daughter to herself:

"Dear me,

"Right now, we're gonna go way back in time and bring out all my feelings no matter how painful or confused; about the time when my mom and dad were separated and then move forward slowly feeling everything again. I'm going to unbury things I've kept secret for years and overcome the pain.

"Before mom and dad got separated, I remember when dad would come home and he would never sleep in bed with mom; he always slept on the couch. Mom seemed to feel rejected and mad. I felt so confused and felt like I had to make things right for them. Dad always kept his feeling so locked up, I never had any idea of what he was feeling. I guess that's the reason I got so close to mom. When dad was home he was always working on something. I always wanted to be close to him but I was scared that if I tried to get him to pay attention to me, he would reject me and I just couldn't handle that. It still scares me.

"The only time, until recently, that I ever felt my dad really loved me was when he gave me jewelry for Christmas or my birthday. I guess that's why, even to this day, I cherish the *things* he's given me. When mom and dad got separated I felt that dad just didn't love us anymore. I didn't feel I was doing everything I possibly could to make my parents love me. I didn't feel I was worth their love. Every time they left to go on the road I felt like such a failure. I hated myself so much for being mad at them for leaving us. When dad left, after they got separated and we moved to Florida, I was so angry at him. I just didn't know how to express it and when I tried telling mom how I felt and it came out as me hating dad, then she got mad and told me she didn't want to hear it. I felt like I wasn't supposed to be angry and I tried all the harder to be sure that anger didn't show. Mom and dad fought an awful lot when they first separated and mom would get off the phone crying. I was really afraid and felt like I would be rejected if I couldn't make mom feel better. My birthday came around during all this mess—dad didn't even send me a card but he did call. I felt it was so necessary to tell him how good I was trying to be. Then mom got on the phone and she and dad had a huge fight. I was so scared. I didn't know how I was going to be able to keep everyone at peace and happy. I felt so guilty as if I hadn't been born on that day none of this would be happening.

"When mom and dad got back together, the first thing she did was run off with dad and leave us with grandma. Needless to say, I worked real hard to make sure everything was perfect so grandma would have no reason to get angry and yell at me or my brothers. She never yelled at my older brothers, because they were always perfect, no matter what they did. I guess I didn't really care how much she yelled at me but I felt I really had to protect my younger brother. I just know she hated him. When we all moved back to Texas everything was okay for awhile. Dad even promised me he would take me on a trip with him. I tried not to get real excited because he would always make some excuse to get out of taking me. He had done it several times in the past. He would always say that mom could really use me at home this time so I would have to decline and he would take one of the boys. As usual, he found a way out of taking me along. I was so hurt and I felt really rejected. When we moved to New York, mom and dad got a job working together and that's when I really started playing the role of the parent. They went to work before we went to school and come home after we went to bed, so I cooked, cleaned, and put the boys to bed. I really resented having to do all this and not being able to have fun like everyone else my age. But I was so scared to tell mom and dad for fear they would no longer love me or even like me for complaining. I got so I would point out things I did just so they would say how nice it was. To me, that was my reward (love).

"When they were home I felt jealous, confused, and scared because then I would have to return to the role of being a child. After awhile, I just stayed in my room and that way I didn't have to face any of those feelings. I finally figured out, though, that when I was sick I could get both my parents' attention. I never really figured this out until now, though. It really hurt to think that I had to stoop to that low a level just to get attention, or maybe it was so I could feel like a little girl that I always wanted to be. I really get so mad and frustrated about that. All this time, unless I was sick, I never talked to dad about my anger toward him, and I certainly didn't want to say anything to mom. I thought if I said anything to dad about it he would reject me and tell me my feelings were wrong, just as mom had. I wanted so much to have a life like my friends and be able to go out on dates and have fun. I really wanted to socialize, but I couldn't because I was afraid to leave mom home alone. I was afraid she would think I didn't love her. Then mom and dad went back to work together and would come home on weekends only. I would then use my brothers as an excuse for not being able to go out. By this time I was really scared of trying to make friends. On the weekends mom and dad came home and once more I would have to play the role of the child. I actually had to ask permission to go out. Sometimes I really felt like going out and never coming back. But I knew that would truly disappoint my parents and I was so scared of losing their love. But I hated myself more and more for being so angry at them and not being able to say that I didn't want to take care of the boys. I really needed to say that I wanted and needed a mom and dad who loved me. I wanted so much to be like everyone else that it actually made me feel pain and emptiness where my heart should be. I felt like I had to act like an adult, but what I really wanted to be was a child. I was so lonely. I always promised myself that I would never be lonely like that when I grew up. It was so scary. But I thought it was all my fault and I really wasn't good enough to deserve any better. To this day, mom and dad both can still control my life with their words and looks. It can make me so angry, confused, and feeling trapped. I wanted to be able to control my own life and have no anger or guilt feelings toward my parents. I don't want to feel lonely or scared then I think they don't love me. I don't want to think I can't live without their love and approval. I want to be able to love me and accept me."

Jan, the mother, and Mary, the daughter, decided to come together for some help with their problems. When Jan came into counseling with her daughter, she stated that she hoped her daughter could talk about her feelings toward her dad; talk out her feelings toward her. Her daughter, at first, was not able to do this but after the letter had been written she began opening up and dealing with a lot of the fears that she had in confronting her mom. Her new outward actions were a good guide that internally Mary was changing. Prior to her coming to counseling, she could not even look in the mirror at herself, without having this terrible, put down feeling. She is now dressing up, wearing make-up, which she has never done in her life. As a result of dealing with her feelings toward her parents, and her feelings toward herself, and as a result of letting herself realize that her parents did love her and would not reject her, Mary finally started becoming Mary.

Mary perceived rejection from her mother and from her father, because both of the parents were very busy trying to deal with their relationship and trying to get their own individual needs met first. Her mother admits that she had difficulty feeling loved by her own parents. Jan admitted that she could have scared Mary off with her temper. It was very difficult for Jan to see that she, at times, entirely pulled away from her daughter. She never stopped loving her daughter, but she did pull away emotionally. The daughter, being young and not knowing what that meant—not knowing the pain her mother might be going through, felt that it was all her fault. She felt that she was to blame for her mother's pain; that her mother did not love her; that her mother was having problems because of her. A total misperception which brought about a lot of pain and a lot of sorrow!

You might be asking yourself, "How do you avoid these misperceptions?" "How do you avoid having your children NOT get into such a situation as mentioned above?" The answer is, "It's not easy!" If, however, we as parents, take the time to tell our children that we love them and do not allow ourselves, as parents, to harbor any hatred or negative feelings toward our children, they won't misperceive our basic message of love.

There is, at times, a subtle movement away from a child by a parent. It's easy for me to say, "Don't do that, because it is harmful!" But the truth is, IT IS HARMFUL!!! Moving emotionally away from your child can have its negative side effects, especially if this is a consistent pattern of behavior on the part of the parent. Occasionally, we will become very discouraged and very frustrated with our children. The key is to not stop loving them! The most interesting part of this is that children can perceive when parents stop loving. It becomes very evident. There is that unspoken feeling of rejection or acceptance that is consciously or unconsciously perceived by the child from a parent. That unspoken rejection, if it occurs too often, can cause problems within the child. You might ask yourself, "How do I avoid this when I'm angry; when I'm frustrated; when I do hate what is going on with my child?" The response to this might be that parents would need to deal with the extremes of their frustration and anger before they begin to deal with their child. Take 5 minutes. Take 10 minutes. Take 15 minutes. If necessary walk away from your child and then go back and deal with him, after you have calmed down and when your emotions are not at such a negative peak. You also may need to allow yourself time to ventilate about some of the frustrations that occur within your family situation. You may choose to do this with a professional therapist, with a minister, with a spouse, or with a friend. Allowing yourself time to reflect and to deal with your emotions can be so very, very beneficial to you, as a parent. Put into perspective your feelings toward your children!

The one factor you should re-emphasize is that you do not accept, nor do you tolerate the unacceptable behavior of your children. You need to learn to focus on applying consequences for the behavior rather than on allowing yourself to get so over emotionally involved in response to that behavior! The anger that you might display toward a child in response to a negative behavior will be remembered by the child as an anger, not as a correction for what the child did. The child will forget why you were angry but he will probably continue to focus on your outward manifestations of that anger. If you keep that in mind, that the emotion will be remembered a lot longer than what you were trying to correct, you will soon learn that you need to correct the behavior with the consequences and remove some of the intense emotion that goes along with this! It is easier said than done, but that is the goal toward which you need to be striving.

I worked with another family where the mother totally denied in any shape or form that she was emotionally rejecting her daughter. The mother denied that this could be happening. She was almost ready to physically, or at least verbally fight me when confronted with the fact that her daughter was very adamant about her rejection. Finally, one day, I got the mother and the daughter together and her daughter told her that she feels that every time she does something wrong, her mother distances herself emotionally, pulls away, won't speak to her, and acts as if she hates her. Her mother got angry and said back to her, "You're lying! That is not true! How can you say those thing about me?" and pouted and got angry and distanced herself! After the third time her daughter told her mother how she felt, the daughter finally broke down and let out so much sorrow that it shocked her mother into realization that she had just done it again. In a moment of truth, the mother broke down and said, "I believe you!" Reality had hit. The mother realized that she had used her love as the only means of control over her daughter and would pull away emotionally. Instead of controlling her daughter it was making her daughter pull away from home—to not care! In fact, her daughter, realized that she had emotionally pulled away from some of her friends like her mother does and was working on correcting this ineffective distancing. This emotional distancing should not be taking place between parent and child. This is my opinion! This is my belief! I have seen it do a lot of emotional harm and a lot of emotional damage. The child, young adult, needs the parent's acceptance. *Acceptance is vital!!* No one can effectively replace the acceptance given by a parent! Children and young adults will grow up and learn to work around their lack of feeling accepted by a parent, but that is far from what that person needs! If you are trying to do things right, as a parent, then you should try to *never* emotionally reject your children. The message is clear, show your emotional support in your child's life. *Your children need you! When they say they don't, they still do!*

Did this chapter seem to key into something within you?

THOUGHTS

- Parents' intentions are good, but the child might not perceive them as such.

- Ask your child how she knows that you love her. The answer could be very interesting and enlightening.

- Yours is the only parental love that your children will ever know and feel.

- Avoid emotional rejection of your child.

- Your child needs your love from birth to death.

5 THE SECOND ABILITY: EFFECTIVE USE OF DISCIPLINE

The second ability, and maybe the key, that a person needs in order to be an effective parent is to know how to use discipline. Again, many think they know the best way to discipline their child and sometimes everybody else's children. Discipline is *how we teach our children to deal with their own behavior*, and how we help them to learn to set limits for themselves. Discipline, like love, involves many different beliefs. We learn discipline, like love, from our parents and from our teachers in school.

Why should we discipline or set limits for our children? The answer is important. In all aspects of life, we learn to control our behavior. We need to control the amount of food we eat, how much we drink, how long we sleep, how much we exercise, with whom we have sexual intercourse, to stop at a stop sign, not to steal, not to kill, how late we arrive at work and on and on. We learned or didn't learn how to restrict our behavior, how to choose when to restrict ourselves. We learned or didn't learn about limit setting as a child. If we failed, we are probably having great difficulty with our own behaviors today. Do you want your child to have difficulty setting his or her own limits as an adult? If not, then the goal of a parent's setting limits on their child's behavior is to teach the child how to make decisions to set his own limits. Parents teach the child to take responsibility for his or her life and for his or her actions as they affect others. Limit setting is much more meaningful than just getting our child to stop embarrassing us in the store when he throws a temper tantrum. By teaching him that his temper tantrum is not an acceptable response to his not getting bubble gum, he will begin to learn, in time, that getting his immediate needs met is not always possible. Limit setting does have a purpose.

Writing about how to deal with a particular child's problem is not an easy task. Before I can begin to give you any ideas regarding discipline techniques to use, I need to convey to you some general concepts about discipline. First, the methods that you choose to use with your child may vary depending on whether you view your child as basically good, bad, or just a child.

Second, you should be consistent with the method of discipline you use. If you do change your approach in discipline, let your children know that you are changing and let them know what the new method is going to be. Do not change approaches without at least two to three week's trial on the old approach. Also be aware that it is possible that you are not appropriately applying the technique to the situation.

Third, be specific about messages and demands that you are placing on your child. Do not assume that the child knows or understands what is expected of him. A good example of this is the case of the mother who told her son to take out the garbage. The son complied with his mother's request but did not meet her expectations. He took out the garbage approximately two minutes before the garbage person arrived in the neighborhood. The mother expected the son to have taken the garbage out before he went to bed the night before. Neither of them had clarified what was meant by the statement, "Take out the garbage."

Fourth, be sure to make the consequence fit the crime. Do not make a consequence, if one is used, either too lenient or too difficult for the misbehavior. Very often parents tend to make the consequence too extreme. An example of an extreme consequence would be placing a tricycle in the garage for three months because the child one time rode the tricycle into the street. Another example would be a parent who hits a child for accidentally spilling a glass of milk.

Fifth, a brief consequence can be and is usually more effective than a consequence that continues too long, especially if the child is young and would forget the reason for the consequence after the first or second day.

Sixth, remember that you are a model for your child. If you are a screamer and cannot stop screaming at your children, they will likely scream in return. I do not believe in the statement, "Do as I say, not as I do." Children will imitate your appropriate and inappropriate behavior. If a child has picked up one of your inappropriate behaviors, one of the first steps that would be helpful *before you discipline the child is to try to control your own inappropriate behavior.*

Seventh, if you use discipline as a means of venting your anger, then the discipline methods will not be very effective. The child will tend to pay attention to the anger and not understand the reason for being disciplined. Parents will become angry, but remember that the method you use is less effective, or not effective at all, when associated with anger.

Eighth, children need to know their limits. It is my opinion that children will behave better when clear and fair limits are set for them and then clearly explained. These limits then become negotiable with age and finally end with the child setting his own limits as an adult.

These are some general ideas about discipline methods. Specific ideas and methods will be presented in the following chapters.

Have you found a key yet? Two keys? Maybe none? I still get excited when I think of people really integrating this key in their life. When you find the key and yet don't feel its significance, then you didn't find it.

THOUGHTS

- Don't be afraid to set limits for your child. They are an absolute necessity.

- Clarity of rules and consistency in enforcement are needed.

- Limit setting helps build self-discipline.

- "The stiffer the consequence the greater the effect" is a false statement.

- You are the model for many of your child's future behaviors.

- Using anger in limit setting only confuses the message to the child.

6 SPANKING: IS THIS A METHOD OR REVENGE?

I feel it is appropriate at this time to deal with an issue of child rearing that has brought about much controversy. That issue is: Should I or should I not spank my child? First, read this statement from a woman who was abused as a child.

"It was 1989 when I first realized the 'spankings' I received during by childhood could be classified as a type of abuse known as corporal punishment. The 'weapons' my family preferred were: my father basically used a belt with buckle or a paddle; my mother preferred her hand to the face or switches to the legs; and my maternal grandmother used barbed wire, screen door springs and belts hitting where ever it landed. I was 'spanked' for everything from crying to being too quiet. My father's favorite thing to 'spank' for was talking back. He would 'spank' you so hard it left marks, and he would 'spank' more if you cried. He would always say he was teaching us a lesson.

"As I grew up, I began to expect 'spankings' as often as I sneezed. So you see, I became so accustomed to 'spankings' that it wasn't a total shock for me to marry a man who also liked the idea of corporal punishment.

"During all these years, I have learned to turn off pain, and not to cry, feelings were not allowed.

"I have also grown up with little respect for people who 'spank' their children. Children do not deserve to be hit in any fashion. Talking, reasoning and explaining does a lot more good. Their fragile minds and bodies can be damaged for life, maybe fatally.

The mental and emotional damage alone is severe. I know you will probably say, 'But I need to teach them a lesson.' Lessons can be taught kindly and lovingly. Please do not beat children. Children are God's gift to us, to love and nurture.

"Love and understanding will do more than 'spanking'."

Spanking is not a creative method of dealing with your children. Spanking is one of the easiest methods to use and requires the least amount of thought. Let me define what I mean by spanking. Spanking, is when a parent uses physical force against the child to show disappointment with the child and to control the child. Spanking can, and often does, carry with it the meaning that the child had better do what she is being told. This in turn generates fear in the child to respond appropriately.

What are the benefits of spanking? Most parents tell me that they like to spank because it is the first thing that comes to mind. Also because it indicates to the child who is in control. Many parents have told me that spanking relieves tension for them as parents. Some have said that spanking was the method their parents used and it worked out of fear. There are many other reasons why spanking could be used, but let's stop for a moment and look at some of the fallacies that exist about spanking.

Spanking is not meant to relieve the tension that builds up in parents when their children don't obey. Any form of discipline should not have as its sole goal, the reduction of parents' tension. The discipline method should carry a lesson. Another fallacy is that children learn their lesson when parents spank. This is not always the case. Very often the children react to the parent's anger rather than reacting to what they did wrong. Often spanking masks the parents' motives for spanking and the lesson it intended to give.

Children have told me that they prefer spanking to some other forms of punishment as it is quick and over with in a matter of seconds.

In my opinion, spanking is an aggressive act and *aggression begets aggression.* I have found that within one to thirty minutes after a child has been spanked, the child himself will react aggressively. The child will probably go find someone else or something else to react to with physical force. In some cases, a child will hit a parent or a sibling or another child who is near them. Another form of reacting to spanking may be that a child will smash a toy or throw an object.

Very often parents use spanking to vent their own frustrations. Parents need to be aware of the reasons why they use spanking instead of some other form of discipline which might more effectively teach a lesson. I have always felt that the purpose of discipline is to teach children how to control their own behavior in society. Discipline is meant to teach children how to make proper decisions regarding their own behavior. Spanking does not teach them a lesson unless time is taken to instruct the child. Other more meaningful methods can be used to explain the improper behavior and what should be done to correct that behavior.

If you do not like for your children to be aggressive, I ask that you consider forms of discipline other than spanking. I'm not sure why you would want your child to be aggressive. You will not beget a "sissy" if you do not use spanking. Remember that as a child grows older and gets bigger, you will not be able to use spanking and will have to change methods at that time. Why not learn different and more effective methods now? And finally, spanking leads to a power struggle. Using spanking shows the child who is more powerful. At some point, the child will find a method to equal the power displayed in spanking. If you wish to control your children, spanking would meet this need.

However, it will cease when the child is physically capable of controlling you. This rebellion to spanking usually takes place during the teen-age years.

As you can tell, I am opposed to using spanking as a primary form of discipline. If another method can be found, I prefer using that method. Using spanking as a rare form of discipline makes it much more effective, if it needs to be used at all. Spanking teaches control. I feel, that in most cases, we should try to teach our children more than just who is in control.

If a child has been psychologically diagnosed as an Attention Deficit Disordered Child with Hyperactivity, the use of spanking as a method of discipline usually increases that child's level of activity. It often stirs the urge to fight or hurt back.

Do you like to be hit? Do you like your body space being physically aggressed upon? How do you react and how do you feel while being hit? The child probably feels the same way. Just because it may have worked for your parents on you doesn't make it a good method to use on your children.

Has something struck a chord yet? Has it *hit* you yet?

THOUGHTS

• "My parents hit me" does not make spanking an effective method to use on children.

• Aggression begets aggression.

• Spanking teaches fear. There is enough fear in the world without creating more.

• Sparing the rod does not create a "wimp."

• How do you increase spanking without beating a child?

7 TIME OUT, TIME IN, NOT AGAIN, TIME OUT

Parents have several choices of methods to use in effectively disciplining their children. Yet the attitude you communicate when you discipline is just as important as the method that you might choose to use. Communication experts state that it is not so much what you say as how you say it. For example, you can say, "No, you cannot do this" in many different ways by varying the style of delivery of the message. You can shout the message. You can say the message with a smile and a very warm look in your eyes. You can turn away from the person when you express the message. There are many other combinations possible. As I outline various methods of discipline, you should remember the importance of how you use them. Be aware of what your body and face are telling your children.

The first method I wish to explain to you is called the Time-Out Method. It is the most commonly used method in dealing with children ages two to twelve, and the most effective overall. This method has also been called the Corner Method, "get your rear in that chair," and just plain "my method." The Time-Out Method is used when you need immediate action in response to the behaviors of your child. The principles behind this method are relatively easy to explain, but as parents tell me, difficult to do in a consistent manner. The general thoughts about this method need to be brought to your awareness. For your first step you need to write down two behaviors of your child that you think are inappropriate. For example, let's say you have a five-year-old who consistently fights with his younger brother. The behavior you would wish to control would be fighting. Another behavior that you might like to see changed would be your child sassing you back when you ask him to do something. For this particular child, the two behaviors you would choose are fighting and sassing.

Your next step is to determine a spot in your house where you will place your child when he behaves inappropriately. This spot needs to be located away from the mainstream of family activity. It should be a quiet place *where the child will get bored.* Parents have used many places when trying to isolate their child. One parent situated the chair in the middle of the room where the child sat during the time-out period. Most parents prefer to use a corner of a room that is away from family activity. When sitting or standing in that chosen spot, the child is not to have any toys, nor should he be able to be entertained with music or television. He should not like the idea of having to go to the corner or the chair.

Now that you have identified the behaviors and chosen the spot where you will send your child when he misbehaves, you need to set the amount of time the child will spend in that spot. I prefer to use only one to ten minutes in the corner for each offense. For example, if the child sasses his father, a predetermined time for this offense should have already been set by the parents. When the father is sassed, the child automatically is to be sent to the corner for that predetermined amount of time. As Johnny sasses his father, his father says, "Johnny, because you have sassed me, you are to go to the corner for five minutes." Dad and Johnny both knew before Johnny was sent to the corner that sassing was to be followed by the predetermined consequence of five minutes in the corner.

Prior to starting this method, it is important to sit down with your children and tell them what you are planning to do. For example, if Johnny was an only child, I would have you call him into the living room and sit down with him to tell him that something new and different is going to begin in your house. The conversation might include the following ideas:

"Johnny, in the past you have been hitting the neighbor boy when he tells you he doesn't want to fight. You have been caught fighting at school by the teachers and you try to fight with us when you are asked to do things that you don't want to do. In the future when you start fighting with the neighbor boy and we see this or when you start fighting with us, we are going to try a new approach with you. We are doing this to try to teach you better ways of acting. (The wording will change depending upon the age of the child.) So from now on when you fight, we are going to place you in the corner (show him) and make you stay there for five minutes. We are doing this so that you will learn to control your fighting by yourself. Johnny, we also know that you tend to sass us back a lot when you don't like things. We are also going to help you try to control your sassing us. By sassing, we mean when you loudly yell at us, 'No, I am not going to do that, you dummy.' (Give as many examples of sassing as you can.) When you sass, Johnny, we are going to help you to stop this by placing you in the corner for five minutes. While you are in the corner, you are to sit there quietly until your time is up. If you are not quiet while you are in the corner, we won't start timing you until you settle down. Do you have any questions about this?"

The above is just an example of a conversation with the child as you begin to introduce this method to him. He may not listen to what you have said, but at least you have informed him of the consequences that will follow should he misbehave.

A good method to measure the time out period is with a sand timer or a cooking timer with a bell. I really like the sand timer best because the child can see the time slip through the glass tubes. A sand timer is also useful because if a child continues to disrupt while he is in the corner, you can quietly turn the sand timer sideways and say to the child, "I am not going to let the sand continue to go through until you have settled down." Then walk away until the child becomes quiet.

I have just explained the basic Time-Out Method. What I need to explain to you now are some of the principles and ideas behind this method. First, it is very important that if you use this method, do so with consistency. It is very important to be consistent because a small child will continue to test you if you reward him by not following though with the consequence for his inappropriate behavior. It would be like my telling you that you cannot have a piece of candy but every once in awhile when you ask I say, "Yes, you may." I may only tell you "yes" once out of every twenty-five times you ask, but the fact that I allow you to have candy once in twenty-five times makes you still ask me the other twenty-four times. If you do not apply the consequences every time, the child will, in all probability, try to get by with that behavior in the future. Once in awhile you might forget or become too busy to always be consistent, but you need to make the effort.

Another point is that Time-Out can reduce the amount of unnecessary arguing between you and your child. Often parents waste time by telling their children five times to *stop doing something* before taking action to try to *stop the behavior*. With this method, the first time you see your child fight or sass or misbehave, you can immediately send the child to the corner with a minimum of interaction. You say to the child, "Johnny, you were fighting. You know the consequences for fighting. Go to the corner for five minutes." Do not argue with your child. Do not get into a lot of disagreements as to what went on. You have made the decision to set consequences for fighting, so be sure to follow though by putting him in the corner.

I have talked about attitude as being very important in every discipline method. In the above method, I encourage parents to be factual and direct with their children when telling them the consequences of misbehavior. That is the beauty of this method. When the child fights, the child immediately goes to the corner. There should not be time for a parent's anger to arise. Anger usually arises after a child has been told numerous times to do something but refuses. With this method, the child is told immediately what to do before the parent gets upset. Even though the words might be the same, I can tell a child to go to the corner in many different styles and with varying emotional contents. I am asking you, as parents, to watch the emotional content of what you tell the child as you apply consequences to his misbehaviors.

Many parents like to warn their children by saying such things as, "If you don't stop fighting, I will send you to the corner." When you do that, the child doesn't know how many times and how many chances he has before Mom means what she says. Consequently, he will try until he finally realizes that she means business. One child told me that it is usually the fourth time Mom tells him that he knows he has reached her limit and he had better obey. The child went on to say that he knew exactly when his mother meant business because her voice got "all funny" and became very high-pitched. Basically, the mother wasted three efforts to control the child. I ask you not to warn your children once they know the consequences that will occur. They also know the behavior is inappropriate because you have talked to them about what they are doing. Therefore, since they know it is inappropriate, you should immediately apply the consequences as stated to them. That might be difficult to do, but it works much more effectively if you follow through immediately every time.

This method of Time-Out can be used with older children, but needs to be modified to their age level. For example, you may consistently ask a teenager to sit quietly for ten minutes and come up with a better way to handle his misbehavior. I do not see this method as being effective with older children because of its simplicity. With this method you are asking for immediate response/choice from the child. Aside from telling the child what you are going to do, you have given the child very little input as to what will happen. With teenagers who are trying to become independent, this method does not allow them any *input* into deciding effective consequences for their inappropriate behaviors. There is probably a better way to work with teenagers than the Time-Out Method. It will be up to you to modify this form based on the age and maturity of your young adult. Your goal is to get the young adult to stop what he is doing and think of a better way of responding.

The Time-Out Method is designed to shape appropriate behaviors which could otherwise have been negative behaviors if left untouched. You are taking a behavior such as fighting and trying to make it an unacceptable alternative for the child. When the child doesn't fight, you continue to shape his behavior by praising him for his use of more acceptable alternatives. Time-Out teaches a child to give up certain behaviors. Parents can offer the child better alternatives and more appropriate ways of acting.

When trying to change inappropriate behaviors, make sure that you define exactly what behaviors you do not like. Explain to the child what you mean by his fighting and what you mean by his sassing. The child might wrestle in a friendly manner with the neighbor boy, but if this consistently leads to fighting, you will have to include this in your definition of fighting. If the child can wrestle with a brother or with his neighbor and keep it friendly, then you may not want to include this in your prohibition against fighting. Another point is the importance of not arguing with your children about who was guilty in starting the negative behavior. If you have several children who know fighting is prohibited, then as the fighting starts, those fighting go to the corner. If you feel a need to discuss with your children what just occurred, do so later. Do not carry on a conversation with them while you are disciplining them. Do communicate with your children often at other times, however. Tell them how they are doing with their behaviors. Be positive with them regarding their not fighting or not sassing. Every child likes to be talked to in a nice way, but if you talk to them during the Time-Out period, they may enjoy it and thereby increase their inappropriate behavior.

Questions will arise when you use this method. You may tend to get frustrated because you have to consistently place demands on yourself to follow through with the consequences. You may feel like screaming or jumping up and down because you have had a lot of pressures that day and do not feel like dealing with your child's misbehaviors. All of these feelings may arise but remember that if you are consistent and persistent in using the method as outlined above, YOU WILL SUCCEED. This method does work and you can make it work for you. Do not give up.

More insights, more ideas have been given to help you be an effective parent. What are your feelings about this chapter? Do you feel the key has been communicated to you?

THOUGHTS

- Time-Out is effective if you understand how to use it.

- Time-Out stops the unacceptable behavior.

- Watch your attitude when you use Time-Out.

- Don't get yourself into the corner by being inconsistent.

- Most children get bored sitting in Time-Out. This is just another reason for them to avoid the inappropriate behavior.

- Consistently try the method for a minimum of two weeks.

8 REWARD APPROPRIATE BEHAVIOR— GOODY GOODY

In the last chapter, we discussed controlling a child's behavior through the use of the Time-Out Method. Another method of discipline is to control a child's behavior through rewarding when he behaves appropriately. That may sound very simple and easy to accomplish; in fact, you might feel that you do this all the time. A lot depends on whether you tend to be positive or negative in your life. The more positive a person you are, the more you will tend to reward and encourage good behavior. As with the last method I described, if you are going to reward appropriate behavior, you must do it consistently.

To apply this method of influencing behavior, you need to select one or two behaviors you wish to see occur more often in your children. For example, if you would like to see more appropriate play between two of your children, you may wish to choose that behavior. If you wish to see better grades from your child, you may wish to select that behavior to develop. Once you have selected those two behaviors, the next step is to sit down with paper and pencil and begin to brainstorm a specific goal and all of the activities that will encourage the reaching of the goal. Let me clarify what I mean by this. If you would like to see better grades from your child, you would list on this sheet of paper the goal you wish your child to reach within a specified time. For example, you would like to see your child receive one letter grade improvement in each subject, except math, within the next grading period. Now that you have stated your goal, you need to brainstorm some of the activities you will reward as your child or young adult climbs the ladder toward the goal. Let me give you some examples. Reward Sally when she brings home a good paper from school. Reward Sally when she begins to read a good book. Praise her when she studies. Continue to encourage her when she asks a friend to help with homework. Listen to her when she talks about her school work. Praise her when she reads the newspaper. Set good examples of reading for her by continuing to read yourself and by talking positively about it.

These are just a few of the activities that can be rewarded to encourage Sally to earn better grades. The list is endless. You should continue to brainstorm to find more behaviors that might lead her to her goal.

For Charlie, the child you would like to see reach the goal of playing more appropriately with his brother, you need to do the same type of brainstorming. For example; you should encourage Charlie by praising him when he does something nice for his brother. You should encourage Charlie or praise him when he's sitting quietly next to his brother. Reward him in some way when he plays for ten minutes with his brother without fighting. Praise him when he shares a toy with his brother. Praise him when he says something nice to his brother.

Again, these are just some examples of the behaviors that you can encourage in Charlie. The list is endless, as it was for Sally.

This method encourages, through reward, a child's steps toward positive ways of acting in life. Some forms of rewarding have already been discussed in the chapter. Below are some others.

1. Praise may be given to your child. Praise consists of words that encourage children to continue doing what they are doing.

2. You may hug your children. You may pat your children on the back. Touch your children in a positive manner.

3. A simple smile may be very rewarding to children.

4. You may reward children with some type of privilege or treat when they have reached an appropriate step in attaining the goal. For example, when brothers don't fight with each other for two hours (or four hours) you may reward their efforts for having attained the two (or four) hour level.

Basically, you can create your own reward for the children depending on what the children consider to be rewarding. Rewards can take many forms and it has as its basis making the child want to repeat an appropriate behavior.

You need to remember to reward behaviors again and again. Be consistent about your efforts to praise the behavior while reminding yourself that rewarding appropriate behavior is very effective. You can become aware of the effects of rewarding behavior by doing the following: prior to starting a system of reward, you should take a tally of how often a certain behavior occurs, such as Charlie playing appropriately with his brother. After you have measured how often Charlie plays appropriately with his brother and have a record of this, you may then begin your systematic efforts of rewarding Charlie's appropriate play. After two weeks of consistently rewarding the behavior, then again measure how often Charlie is playing appropriately with his brother. There should be an increase. Behaviors can continue to grow and increase through your encouragement.

This method can be systematized more effectively with smaller children through the use of a chart. Place on the chart two, three, or four behaviors that you would like to see occur more often in your children. These behaviors are written so the child can understand them. You then make little boxes on the chart where you can place some form of mark, star, or smiling face. Each time the child performs this behavior, you make a consistent effort to reward that behavior by placing the mark, star, or smiling face on the chart. This is done in the presence of the child at least once a day. This chart works well for small children as they like to see smiling faces or stars. The chart method also makes the parents more aware of their plan to reward certain behaviors.

Rewarding appropriate behavior is effective. I do not know a single person who does not like to be rewarded for his efforts. Being positive with your child has much more meaning to the child than always trying to control the child through negative means. Try this method if you already haven't. I feel you will like it. I feel your child can key into this method!

THOUGHTS

- Being positive is much more effective than being negative.

- Most children/people like to know that what they do is appreciated.

- Make an effort to not only praise your children, but also your spouse and other important people in your life.

- There is so much good in people, please look for it.

- Don't overlook your own good.

9 LET IT HAPPEN—BE BRAVE—SOMETIMES

Children tend to perform a behavior and then look to see what the results are going to be. Children are not always aware of doing this, but they are aware if consequences do or do not follow from what they just did. For example, a four-year-old girl goes into the room next door and sees her younger brother playing with a toy that she likes. She immediately decides she wants to play with that toy. She grabs the toy away from her brother and returns to another room. As she does this, she is somewhat aware of the fact that the last time she snatched a toy from her brother, he screamed and she got into trouble. The little girl is aware that she could be in trouble again for taking the toy from her brother but she decides to go ahead and try, hoping that she gets the toy and can play with it without her mom and dad making her give it back to her brother. If nothing happens to her and if she succeeds in getting away with this behavior, you can bet your bottom dollar that she will try this again. Being able to play with the toy without suffering any consequences was a reward to her. Nothing happened.

There are certain behaviors which automatically bring consequences. A very good example would be if you drop a five-pound rock on your toe, your toe is going to hurt. If you touch a hot stove, you will burn your finger. In dealing with children, there are certain consequences that are effective deterrents to a child performing a behavior again. Sometimes these natural results are excellent means of controlling a behavior. What a parent must decide is whether or not the results that naturally follow would be appropriate, too severe, or have no effect at all on the child. Allowing a child to burn his finger would be too severe, but allowing him to feel the hotness of something that does not burn him would be a lesson in not touching certain items that are hot. There is no way you can always be around your children to protect them from harmful experiences in their lives. The consequences of certain events will influence your children without your being aware of it. Children tend to remember these consequences as they get older.

I am not advocating that you let a child experience only natural consequences, but I do encourage parents to allow certain harmless natural consequences to take place if those consequences will help a child learn the boundaries of behavior. The natural consequence, such as letting a child stay up later after many attempts to get him to bed, may be particularly effective for this child when he must arise at 6:30 the next morning to get ready for school. Some children will learn that staying up late only makes them miserable the next day. Other children will not learn from this type of natural consequence and, therefore, I would not encourage parents to use this method with those children. Trial and error is the only way you can tell if your children will benefit from a particular natural consequence. Your effectiveness in teaching your children early in their lives that there are consequences to their actions will greatly enhance their ability to control their behavior.

Some consequences are not so natural but can be used to bring about change in your child. If you set up certain contingencies or certain consequences for specific behaviors and make these clear to the child, you will find these behaviors will begin to change. Let's take some examples. If a child leaves his clothes on the floor and refuses to pick them up, you set the consequence with him that only clothes in the hamper will be washed. The result is that clothes that are left on the floor do not get washed. When it is time to go to school and his favorite sweat suit or shirt is not washed, he will soon begin to feel the consequences of not putting the clothes in the hamper. The consequence follows from setting up the rule that clothes not in the hamper do not get washed. If your child cares about what he wears to school, this rule will be effective. If your child does not care whether he wears clean or dirty clothes to school, then you have another problem. This problem may be indicative of a lack of personal hygiene values, poor self-esteem, or a child who at this stage in his development does not care how he looks to others.

Another example of consequences being set and letting the result cause change in the child is to not allow a child to eat dinner when he arrives home late. Some children simply refuse to come home on time when playing with their friends after school. Assuming the child is old enough to tell time, you let the child know when he is expected home for dinner. When that time arrives and dinner is ready, you begin with or without him. If he comes home after dinner is over, you tell him he missed dinner and he will have to eat what is left and clean up the dishes or he will have to wait until morning for breakfast. Caution—do not overdo this consequence. Missing a meal very often can be physically unhealthy. I do need to caution you to at least ask the child why he was late. There might have been something that was a legitimate excuse. This would probably be the exception rather than the rule. I can guarantee you the child will not be late very often if he knows he will have to eat leftovers and do dishes or he will miss dinner if he does not arrive at home on time.

Sometimes the child's problem does not relate directly to the home or the parents. For example, a child may have a problem with picking fights with others at school. Everywhere else the child seems to behave himself reasonably well. It is very possible that this fighting at school will be handled either by the school officials or by a bigger kid who finally wins the fight with your child. The consequence of getting beaten by a bigger kid may stop your child from fighting in the future. In these cases, there might be a chance the child will learn his lesson from other people or other consequences without the parents' involvement. As the child gets older, very often teachers, peers, administrators, counselors, and special adults will influence and bring about change in your child.

There is a maturity that needs to take place within children as they become young adults. This maturity helps children see how their own misbehavior will lead to results that are displeasing to them to such a degree that they will willingly control their own behavior. The children mature through proper guidance of the significant adults around them. They learn that their behaviors result in consequences. They are taught by adults what happens when certain behaviors are performed. Children without this maturity have problems later on in life. Many, for instance, never learn that their behaviors produce consequences that negatively affect their lives and the lives of others.

Natural and logical consequences are not the only methods of dealing with the child's behavior, but these methods can be very effective if used consistently, explained to the child, and enforced accordingly.

Naturally, certain consequences will follow certain behaviors. Logically, we can set up certain consequences to occur if a child does something we do not wish him to do. Consequences are important and, if tailored to the individual child with his wants and needs, will be useful in helping the child to behave properly.

Can you see this method working in your family setting? Can you adapt this method in any way to bring about a change in a family member? Are you keying in?

THOUGHTS

- Certain behaviors have their own consequences which naturally follow the act.

- Try to make your consequences logically fit the behavior. e.g. Talking on the telephone too long can mean reduction in telephone use the next day.

- Do not assume your child understands your logic. Explain it.

- Do not forget to reward the positive behaviors that occur.

- Keep a healthy attitude toward your child.

10 CHILD INVOLVEMENT IN LIMIT SETTING

I have mentioned several ways to discipline your child. Many unexplored ways exist to deal with behavior. One method that has not been mentioned is to have the child develop his own discipline with parental assistance. This particular method of child involvement requires parents to assume that their children are capable and willing to be involved in their own self-betterment. Parents who use this method will need to assume that their children want to consciously do what is right and are somewhat self-motivated toward achieving that goal. The underlying purpose of this method is to teach children that they can and will eventually be responsible for their own discipline and self-control as adults. This is an idealistic concept but in many cases can be made very realistic.

Parents would like to see their children grow up and become productive citizens. Parents would like to help their youngsters make correct decisions in life and want to watch their children become adults who are capable of living effectively in our society without hurting themselves or others because of wrong decisions. Involving the young children in making some appropriate decisions regarding behaviors will help them develop into effective adults. You can help children become effective adults by asking their input in matters of discipline as well as everyday living concerns.

Many obstacles arise in the minds of parents when they consider involving children in discipline matters. Parents might be afraid that their children will want to control them if they are given a say in discipline matters. Parents might feel their children will be too lenient on themselves if they are allowed input into their own discipline. Parents could be afraid they will lose control if they do not enforce what they believe is right. Some parents do not believe children have any good thoughts regarding their own discipline. Finally, some parents believe that children will be out only for themselves and will not be concerned about others in the family. In response to these concerns, it is evident that not all children will cooperate with parents in trying to set their own discipline. In time, however, most children will become involved in trying to help themselves behave better within the family structure if the appropriate attitude is set within the household. Basically, to make this method work, the cooperation of every family member is needed. Fortunately, children do not have to remain self-centered and concerned about only their own well-being. You can teach children to become responsible for their own behavior. Granted, it may be very difficult, especially with children who have been spoiled or who have had control of the family for quite some time. Some children have learned how to manipulate their parents almost from the first cry after they were born. That is somewhat exaggerated but some children do know how to work their parents to the point where the child is in control and the parents work desperately to regain that control.

Let's start at the beginning. The beginning involves asking your children to cooperate and be willing to try a new method of dealing with their inappropriate behavior. Getting children to willingly try to work on their negative behavior is the key to making this approach work. I have found that children tend to balk at this method if they feel they are going to lose ground in controlling their parents, or if they will not have continued success in getting their way. Many times, giving children the option of having a say in the discipline methods rather than having the parents do whatever they so wish with discipline makes children really think about the two choices available. When given that choice of being involved or of their parents having total say, the children often will choose to become involved.

Once you have gotten your children involved with you in working out some consequences for their agreed upon ineffective behaviors, you are on the way to success. Cooperation usually ends up with successful results. What you are asking your children to do is help you set some consequences on specific behaviors they perform that cause you to feel that your rights are being violated.

How do we go about involving the child in discipline? Basically, you need to choose several behaviors that are a problem for this particular child. You then sit the child down with you for a long talk regarding these behaviors. You need to state that these behaviors are a problem for you and that these behaviors are affecting the smooth running of the family. You need to continue to encourage the child to cooperate in solving these behaviors. Next, you list the behaviors that are a problem, but do not choose too many to work on at one time. In fact, I feel that to work on more than two or three behaviors at one time would be overwhelming to the child.

Select one of the three behaviors that you wish to help the child control. Take that behavior and brainstorm various ways that might be implemented to help the child change this behavior. List many possible methods of control during this session. Leave nothing unexplored. Creativity is very important at this time. For example, a child has a problem with fighting with his brother. The parents and child brainstorm many possible means to help that child control that behavior. List every thing that is suggested. This list can be written on a blackboard, on a piece of paper, or on a special chart that you might devise for these brainstorming sessions. A child may suggest that he should go to his room for three hours every time he fights. Another child with a different family might state that she should go to her room for five minutes whenever she fights. Yet other children may state that they should be spanked or be put in the corner or not given dinner. No matter what is stated, it should be recorded as an option.

The parents then need to list their suggestions on how the child might learn to behave. One set of parents may suggest sending the child to the corner for ten minutes. Another set of parents may suggest spanking the child. After these suggestions have been listed, it will then be up to the parents and the child to pick one method that they all agree upon as the method that will be tried in the future. In some cases, it may take anywhere from fifteen minutes to two hours to agree upon a solution that is acceptable to both the parents and to the child. In a very few cases, you may have to stop the session and come back to the problem the next day because of lack of agreement. This is usually the exception and I would recommend that a solution be agreed upon during the first session.

Now that a solution to the problem behavior has been chosen, the family members need to agree that they will come back in two weeks to review how the method is working. During the coming two weeks, the parents enforce the newly established consequences with the child. At the end of the two weeks, the family meets again and discusses the effectiveness of the consequences. The child is involved in this discussion. If the child and the parents agree that a new solution should be tried because of the ineffectiveness of the method chosen, then they need to get out the original list to pick a different solution. I would recommend that the parents wait at least two weeks before changing solutions, and there should be valid objections before solutions are changed. If the child wishes to change, but the behaviors are decreasing, you need to point out to the child that the method seems to be working. I am not asking that the child like the consequences, because that is not the goal. The goal is to have the unwanted behavior decrease. There are some children who will want to continue to change solutions for no valid reason. Remember that parents have just as much say as the child in the choice of a solution and its being changed. There must be agreement between the parents and the child before a solution is changed, just as both must agree to the original solution.

When a child refuses to set consequences for a behavior, then you will have to use a method other than child involvement. At this point, go back to one of the other methods described in this book and follow that method with your child. Later, you may want to check out your child to see if he will cooperate in this method of helping himself to control his own inappropriate behaviors.

Parents do not have to agree to try any solution that they feel is not suitable for their child. Both parents and children must be in agreement to try the new consequences. With this method it is also important to remember that children are very intelligent. They are capable of helping themselves with control, especially if they are properly encouraged. Input from your children can make them feel that they are a part of their own destiny. It gives them a sense of responsibility. It helps them believe in themselves. You are not a weak parent if you involve your children in determining consequences for inappropriate behaviors. This method does not differ from others in that *consequences are set* for a child's inappropriate behavior. What you will probably find out is that many consequences you used in the past were not very effective. Brainstorming by the child and the parents brings to light new and better consequences that are more effective.

The purpose for the input from the child in this method of discipline is not for the child to control or rule the parents, but to help him realize that since he is going to be held responsible for his behavior, he might as well be involved in helping to control his own weaknesses. This method is also paving the way for the child to someday be responsible for all of his actions and to control himself.

Finding acceptable methods of controlling the behaviors of children by involving the children in the solution is easier if positive ways of behaving are among the children's choices. For example, fighting will be punished as agreed upon by the parents and children. The children might also be encouraged to share the toy rather than fight, or encouraged to tell the other child, "I do not fight to solve a problem." The suggestion of positive ways of acting should be discussed with the children well before and well after the fighting occurs. Finding a way to influence behavior is important. More important for children is knowing appropriate ways to act in order to avoid ineffective behaviors.

You have now been given ways to help set limits with your children. Some methods will work for your family and others won't. One possible reason for methods working or not working could be the way they are presented. Another possible reason involves the individual differences in children. Part of these individual differences are in the form of temperaments which are the focus of the next chapter. Are you still searching for the key?

THOUGHTS

- Children can learn to set limits on their actions.

- Involving children in finding solutions is a healthy activity.

- Cooperation is a better value than responding out of fear or force.

- Self-control needs to be taught; it is not an inborn response.

- What you expect from children is often what you get.

11 TEMPERAMENTS— HAND ME DOWNS

What has become known to researchers over the years is that the inborn traits of a child which can be loosely called temperaments are a very important factor in understanding children's problems. I am intentionally not going to define temperaments or describe what I mean by inborn traits. I feel the definition will only confuse the issue. The important concept is that children are born with predispositions toward behaving in certain ways based upon qualities that they have received genetically/biologically from the parents. Within the same family there will be children with various traits even though all were treated equally by their parents. Yet, these children, even though they are treated the same, turn out to be different than other siblings living within the same family. In being a parent you are going to realize that you will have to deal with each child individually, based on *who* that child is and based on the particular characteristics of *that child*. Don't fool yourself into trying to believe that all your children will turn out the same. There are many other factors involved besides parenting that influence the behavior of a child. Notice I used the word influence. We shouldn't blame the biological characteristics that children receive from their parents for the way they behave. It is also necessary to look at the environment that helped shape those characteristics in childhood, through adolescence, and into adulthood.

I am going to give you my version of what I interpreted from a study by Dr. Stella Chess and Dr. Alexander Thomas in a book called <u>Origins of Evolution of Behavioral Disorders from Infancy to Early Adult Life</u>.[3] This book studied 133 people from 84 families from birth through a period of about 25 years. The data that they collected was extremely viable as a longitudinal study. What does that mean? It means that they studied people from birth through a period of 25 years rather than having studied someone's behavior for a period of a couple of weeks or a couple of months. What they found is that there were temperaments in children that fit into nine areas. These temperaments seem to play a role in the child's behavior. Chess and Thomas explained temperament as the "how" of behavior, motivations being the "why" of behavior, and abilities being the "what" of behavior. They give examples of two children dressing themselves with equal skillfulness or being able to ride a tricycle with the same dexterity and they also possessed the same models for these behaviors; or two adolescents display similar learning ability and intellectual interest and their goals for the future may coincide; or two adults may show the same degree of abilities in their work and have the same reason for devoting themselves to their jobs, yet these children, these adolescents, and these adults may differ significantly with regard to their quickness with which they move, the ease with which they approach a new physical environment, social situations or tasks, and the effort required to distract them when they are absorbed in an activity. In other words, their abilities and motivations can be very much alike, but their temperaments can be different. Chess and Thomas established the following nine categories of temperament that they found in the children in their case studies:

1. "Activity Level: the motor component present in a given child's functioning and the diurnal proportion of active and inactive periods.

2. Rythmicity (Regularity): the predictability and/or unpredictability in time of any biological function.

3. Approach or Withdrawal: the nature of the initial response to a new stimulus, be it a food, toy,

place, person, etc. Approach responses are positive, whether displayed by mood expression (smiling, verbalizations, etc.) or motor activity (swallowing a new food, reaching for a new toy, active play, etc.). Withdrawal reactions are negative, whether displayed by mood expression (crying, fussing, grimacing, verbalizations, etc.) or motor activity (moving away, spitting new food out, pushing a new toy away, etc.).

4. Adaptability: responses to new or altered situations. One is not concerned with the nature of the initial responses, but with the ease with which they are modified in desired directions.

5. Threshold of Responsiveness: the intensity level of stimulation that is necessary to evoke a discernible response, irrespective of the specific form that the response may take or the sensory modality affected.

6. Intensity of Reaction: the energy level of response, irrespective of its quality or direction.

7. Quality of Mood: the amount of pleasant, joyful, and friendly behavior; as contrasted with unpleasant, crying, and unfriendly behavior.

8. Distractibility: the effectiveness of extraneous environmental stimuli in interfering with or altering the direction of the ongoing behavior.

9. Attention Span and Persistence: two categories which are related. Attention span concerns the length of time a particular activity is pursued by the child. Persistence referred to the continuation of an activity direction in the face of obstacles to its continuation."[3]

In an attempt to understand what Dr. Chess and Dr. Thomas meant by their definitions, I have written some questions that may explain more clearly their categorization of these temperaments. You may use these questions as guidelines to help you discern the difference between the various temperaments in your children and to make you aware that your children will vary on certain temperamental functions.

1. *Activity Level*—I have defined this as being active or inactive, as being busy or not busy, as always doing something or doing nothing. Children will vary as to how long a time they can spend on activities of interest and the types of activities that they will spend time on whether it will be TV, sports, or reading. Many children do nothing and many children are always doing something and some are right in the middle as far as activity level. Children will vary on this factor. There are several questions that might help you look at your child's activity level and look at the variation among your children with regards to this trait. a) How long a time does your child or young adult spend on activities of interest to him or her? Is it 10 minutes, 30 minutes, 60 minutes, or over an hour? b) Does your child or young adult spend most of this time in TV or sitting games, sports like soccer or football, reading, sleeping? c) What percentage of your child's time is spent in doing nothing or doing something? These questions will help you determine activity level.

2. *Rhythmicity*—I have defined rhythmicity as the regularity or non-regularity in a child's biological function such as sleep patterns, bowel patterns, eating patterns. As can be noted, some children

are predictable in their biological functions and some are not. Questions that might help you deal with rhythmicity are: a) Does your child like to be fed on schedule? b) Are there consistent patterns of feeding, sleeping, and napping with your child?

3. *Approach/Withdrawal*—I define this as slow or quick to warm up to new people, to new food, to new a place. It basically is the nature of the initial response of the child to a new stimulus from the outside world. Some questions that may help you understand this approach/withdrawal within children are as follows: a) When presented something new, like a toy, does your child react by smiling and reaching for the toy, or by crying, fussing, and pushing the toy out of the way? b) When taken to new places does your child generally react by smiling, showing contentment, and being at ease, or does your child frown, fuss, withdraw, and try to move away from the new place? c) When presented with new food or a new person does your child accept the food or person, smile and be pleasant, and move toward the person or food, or does your child react negatively and withdraw, frown, or fuss?

4. *Adaptability*—By adaptability we are focusing on whether a child can adapt or not to new situations, new directions, or new directives. Several questions that might help discern what is meant by adaptability are as follows: a) Does your child learn from his/her experience easily? b) Does your child learn from his/her mistakes? c) Is your child able to handle change in ways of doing things, or changes in daily routines that you may impose upon him/her?

5. *Threshold of Responsiveness*—This deals with the intensity of stimulation needed to get a noticeable response from the child. Several questions might help you understand this better. They are: a) Do you need to shout before your child responds? b) Do you need to spank very hard rather than swat easily with your hand before your child responds (if that is the method that you use with your child)? c) Does your child easily notice slight changes around the house, such as a plant being moved; or does your child need a major change before he/she notices, such as all the furniture being moved in a room? d) Is your child easily distracted by noise around him, such as a door slam?

6. *Intensity of Reaction*—Some children need more intense stimulation to get them to react, some react more intensely on their own. The energy level of the response of the child is what we are concerned with in this temperament. a) Does your child usually react to situations mildly and calmly, or with a lot of action and intensity? b) Is your child generally calm, or is you child excitable in response to most situations?

7. *The Quality of Mood*—Moods in children vary. Some are pleasant and joyful, some are very unpleasant, unfriendly, and crying. Several questions might help. a) Is your child usually pleasant, friendly, happy; or is your child unpleasant, crying, and unfriendly? b) Can you describe the type of mood that your child usually displays?

8. *Distractibility*—Is your child easily distractible? The effect of any outside stimuli on your child that might interfere with the direction that your

child is taking is the concern of distractibility. Several questions might help you. They are as follows: a) Can your child read a book and listen to music and yet understand what he/she is reading? b) Do outside noises/voices usually distract your child, or does your child continue to work and play even though many things are going on around him or her?

9. *Attention Span*—Some can work in an activity for a short or long period of time. This is the focus of attention span, the length of time an activity is pursued by a child. A good test for you would be to name three activities that your child engages in and then state the length of time usually spent on those activities. Along with attention span is persistence, which is the continuation of an activity in the face of obstacles to continuing. A question you might need to ask yourself as a parent is: Will your child continue to pursue an activity despite obstacles put in his way? e.g., Will your child continue to try something, even though he is told he doesn't have the skill.

The questions and the explanations that I gave to the nine temperaments as stated by Dr. Chess and Dr. Thomas are my interpretations of these temperaments. These may not be totally accurate according to the dictates of the research of Dr. Chess and Dr. Thomas, but the questions were presented to you so that you might be able to better understand some of the differences within the various children of your family. If your child seems to vary in one of these temperaments, it is at least helpful to be aware that part of the variation is due to heredity, and part to learning.

In dealing with children and their temperaments, it is important for parents to allow the child to express these differences in ways that positively use these qualities. A child who has a high activity level should be allowed to exert a lot of energy in physical activities rather than making reading his predominant mode of physical expression. As a parent it is helpful to be aware of differences within children. Strive to use the child's temperament in reaching a positive end rather than trying to totally change the child's temperament for the sake of conformity or your own personal comfort. Some examples follow:

- Do not require a child with a high activity level to sit and study in one time frame as long as a child with a low activity level. Break up the continuous study time and allow some physical exertion.

- Be more patient with the child who is slow to warm up to people. Give the child more positive feedback for his slightest attempt to interact with people.

- Allow more time for a child who is slow to adapt to learn the change in the daily routine. Tell this child well in advance of any impending changes, and slowly work toward the completion of the change using small steps. For example, if the child is to change schools, first tell him of the change months ahead. Take the child by the school, then go into the school to look around, and then arrange to meet a teacher or some of the students in the school, etc.

- Learn, as a parent, that your intensity may be too strong for your child who needs very little intensity for him/her to react. Also understand that some of your children do not respond to a very low-keyed request.

- Be aware that one of your children may have inherited the temperamental disposition to react with a lot of "gusto." You need to learn how to help him/

her express this "gusto" appropriately. It may also be helpful, as the parent, to learn your own control in response to the "gusto" presented to you.

• A child who is easily distractible needs a quiet place to study. Another child may be able to study with a radio on. When talking to an easily distractible child, make sure you have eye contact.

• A child with a short attention span needs help from you in extending by small segments the time they focus on a task. Be aware of this difference in your children and break up the time required on tasks at home according to the ability to attend to the task.

Temperaments will vary and so should parents' expectations on the child. Once you are aware of these differences in your children, react accordingly. Environment can alter these temperaments, but don't expect any big changes in a short period of time. Helping your child attend to a task will take time, depending on his temperament. Don't rush in, but don't rush away in helping him/her alter this behavior.

To sum up, expect temperamental differences in your children. Help them modify and use these differences in ways that are meaningful to them. Work at a pace that seems to assist each child in change rather than frustrate the child. Most importantly, turn the temperamental quality into a positive characteristic for the child. Again, be creative.

Does this information help you find some missing and needed ingredient in parenting your child?

---

3   Chess, Stella, and Alexander Thomas. Origins and Evolutions of Behavior Disorders. 1984. Brunner/Mazel, NY.

THOUGHTS

- Children within a family do vary and some of the variance is due to temperamental qualities.

- When possible, accept these differences in the child and emphasize the positive aspects of the temperament.

- Your child does not have to be just like you in order to succeed in this world.

- When temperaments are self-destructing to the child, then begin a very positive, step-by-step plan to help the child reduce the ineffective behavior by initiating a more effective response.

- Realize that many of your children's temperaments are handed down to them through you or your spouse.

- Most importantly, realize that people are different and that differences do not have to be negative.

12 EXPECTATIONS— WHAT DO YOU WANT?

Every one of us is expected to do certain things. Your parents had certain expectations of you. Your boss has expectations of you. Your spouse expects certain things of you. Your friends look at you in a certain light and view you as a certain type of person who will behave in certain ways. People who know you generally expect you to behave according to their preset notions of you. Everybody, without exception, has at least one or more persons who place them in a category that assumes certain behaviors. Tom is expected to be on time for work by his boss. The secretary expects him to greet her with a smile and a cheerful, "Good morning." As the day progresses certain job expectations must be met. Tom's friend is expecting him for lunch. His wife wants him to stop by the store on the way home and pick up some milk. Finally, his kids want him to spend some time with them when he comes home from work. I'm sure there are many more demands on Tom than those that were mentioned. Since we all have expectations placed upon us, we need to be aware of the demands we place on others. More specifically, since this book is dealing with parenting, we need to be aware of the demands we place on our children.

We need to know a few things about expectations. It is easy for parents to have set goals that are too high for their children. Also, parents may not expect enough from them. Like most situations, too much or too little is a bad thing. Too great a demand of our children will make them give up and become frustrated because they cannot succeed. Too little an expectation does not produce a challenge and often the child fails to be motivated to complete the task. So, as parents, we need to find a level of expectation for our children that is attainable, and yet high enough to motivate them.

Let's go over a few basic ideas about setting an expectation. First of all, they need to be stated very clearly, in terms a child could understand. They need to be made very specific. An expectation that is stated in terms such as, "I want you to be a good boy," is too vague. A parent who tells a child to behave when he goes over to a friend's house is also being unclear and nonspecific. Most parents tell me that they have repeated over and over what they want from their child. I basically agree with this, but I encourage parents to ask their children to repeat what they feel is expected of them by their parents. If the child can tell you specifically what is expected of him when he goes to a friend's house, then you don't need to drill instructions into him each time he goes.

An expectation needs to be attainable. Children need to be able to see, feel, and hear success in meeting the expectations placed upon them. It is a very sad situation when goals are too high to achieve. If the task can be accomplished by the children with reasonable time and effort, then the goal should be considered attainable. It might be beneficial to use other children and other family situations to help you set reasonable and attainable goals for your children. Astute parents will be able, in time, to read their children's reactions to what is expected of them. When expectations are too difficult to obtain, stress, anxiety, and depression are all possible reactions that can be detected in a child. When the parents see negative reactions occurring, they need to re-evaluate what they want from the child. In some cases, however, it may not be the level of expectation that is the problem, as depression, anxiety, and stress have many causes.

Like discipline, expectations can be forced on children or the children can set some of their own. Like discipline, at some point in the children's lives, they should begin to set and form their own personal levels of expectations. As adults, we often achieve only what we want ourselves to achieve. Establish in your children an attitude that personal goals can be rewarding and meaningful.

I write about expectations because I have seen some children suffer due to unattainable demands. I have also seen children suffer because no one really cared what they did or what they achieved. Again, either extreme can be damaging to children. The child whose parents place too high an expectation on him generally states to me, "If I can't please them, why should I try?" This feeling can result in a very serious problem as I have seen children go from being an "A" student to an "F" student.

When a child meets a parent's expectations or begins to accomplish, I ask that parents praise the child. Parents should teach children how to be happy and enjoy the attainment of their goals. For instance, Johnny is trying to get an "A" in math. The parents know that Johnny is capable of this because they have talked with his teacher. The parents then need to praise Johnny as he attempts to get the "A" in math. The parents should praise him when he studies at home. They should praise any good papers he brings home. The parents should show Johnny how to take time to celebrate his accomplishment. They might suggest that Johnny take a night off from studying math after he brings home a report card with a good grade. The child should take time to enjoy the success of his efforts in attaining his goals.

Another word of caution—you should avoid trying to have your children fulfill your unfulfilled desires. Your children are different from you. Expectations need to be tailored to the individual child. You can best help your child by offering him various opportunities to develop himself. Encourage, persuade, and in some cases, tell your children to try and achieve goals that seem difficult. *Goals for childre n should be beneficial to their future, not yours.*

The basic idea is to encourage children and offer them opportunities to develop themselves. Parental enthusiasm while children are involved in trying out these opportunities helps them to continue their efforts. There is a fine line between strong encouragement and pushing your child too hard to try an activity. REMEMBER THAT POSITIVE ENCOURAGEMENT IS BETTER THAN NEGATIVE FORCE. The fact I keep in mind is that a financially successful but unhappy life is not worth the price. Success is not to be defined totally in monetary terms. Success involves an internal feeling of happiness in what we are doing. *Fulfilling expectations without eventually believing in them will not bring happiness nor success.*

Where do expectations fit into your key to success, and how are your children responding to your expectations of them?

THOUGHTS

- Your expectations of your children need to be in line with their abilities.

- Do not make your child fulfill your own unmet expectations.

- Appropriate expectations can become motivators.

- Expectations are too high when stress, anxiety, depression, or rebellion begin to be expressed by your child.

- As a personal note: Achieve what you wish, but expect nothing in return and you will be happy.

13 DO I REALLY UNDER-STAND MY ATTITUDE?

We spend so much time trying to find out how to do things; how to fix this, how to fix that, how to take care of this problem or that problem. Once we learn how to take care of something or someone, we often feel our task is done. We sit back hoping the "how to" works. Sometimes it does, sometimes it doesn't work, and we then become frustrated after blaming the "how to" information.

What ingredient is often missing in being successful in accomplishing a task? What is often overlooked in trying to successfully deal with people. Attitude is the answer. "I'm aware of that", might be the reply. But are you *really* aware of your attitude? I challenge you to go ask at least ten people you know will be totally honest with you, what they see as your attitude about yourself, your family, your friends, and your work. More importantly, ask your boss, your spouse, your children about your attitude toward them. Do they see areas that need improvement? When you want something done, what is your attitude when you ask them to do this job or chore? Become aware of your innermost feelings when you interact with people. This attitude that you discover or rediscover plays an important role in your life, and in particular, in your dealings with your children. It is easy to feel that your attitude is appropriate. The young lady who wrote the following letter to her mother indicates the misperception of attitude among family members. People's intentions may be good when interacting with others, but what is perceived by the other is what is believed by them.

Attitude is very difficult to accurately express. A young lady puts it very succinctly when she writes in a letter to herself, the attitude she felt her parents expressed toward her when she was growing up.

"At first, I knew my mom loved me because she let me follow her around. I was her pal. But as I grew older she became more angry, less tolerant. She was overwhelmed with home, kids, dad, and work. Mostly you just left her alone. My dad wasn't around much that I remember. When he came home we would eat dinner and he would take a nap. We all had to be quiet. You were rewarded for being quiet; not causing trouble; not asking too many questions. The reward was when they felt like it, they would deal with you...My dad didn't really like us as teenagers. He even has said so on occasions. But as I grew older, about thirteen or fourteen, I learned the way to get attention from him was to do things for him. You have 'to do' to get. If I brought him something he asked for I was a 'good girl;' if I didn't, he didn't really talk to me. I decided that's how I would finally get his attention; I would *do* and he would *give*. I don't know if he figured it out also, but ever since I was about sixteen, he now turns to me to fill a need. He has me pick him up, go with him to shop, come over and visit when mom is gone, call me on the phone and tell me all about his day...

"Though I always probably knew it, my father is an alcoholic. It took me a long time to admit that. I really only acknowledged it 2-3 years ago. My father didn't have time for me because that would take time away from his drinking. He knows I can't stand it also. I guess he doesn't want the guilt. It's hard to love someone when you don't like yourself; when you hide your real self; when you become self-centered and try to overcompensate for the alcohol by becoming self-righteous, intolerant, and hiding behind your religion. That is, of course, how I could get my dad's love—go back to church. Then I would be someone. I often think of the song, *What Have I Got to Do to Make You Love Me? What Do I Have to Do to Be Heard?* I don't know anymore. I just know I'm tired of waiting. I'm not going to get love without doing something first, and that hurts. Your dad is *supposed* to love you! Why doesn't mine? The alcohol, I say, but I don't know...So many conditions. What ever happened to 'I love you, you're my child?'"

The word 'attitude' is very difficult to define. Webster's New Collegiate Dictionary gives two definitions. The first is, "the arrangement of the parts of the body or figure: POSTURE." The second definition is, "a mental position with regards to a fact or state; a feeling or emotion toward a fact or state." Before I had looked at the dictionary definition of attitude, I had in my mind the thoughts that I wanted to convey to the reader. What I was very glad to see was that the definition of attitude started by saying that it is a posture, which is a physical, bodily expression. The arrangement of the parts of the body or figure were stressed over a mental state. *What is important to keep in mind is that an attitude as expressed by somebody is much more non-verbal than it is a verbal statement.* Attitudes are expressed not only by words, which seems to be the most common belief, but also by body posture, such as the motion of the body, whether it's smooth or erratic or rhythmic. It is expressed by voice tone, whether it be melodic or raspy or grating. It is expressed through the tempo of your voice. It is expressed through eye movements, whether they be rapid or a fixed stare. Even breathing patterns express attitudes. These are not often thought of as common conscious ways of communication. They are common ways of expressing attitude, but they are often not brought to our conscious mind.

A good example of what I am talking about happened with Frank and Mary who come into counseling with an entire family of children. They were concerned that their children were not responding to their commands to obey them. The children seemed not to be listening to them. When commands were given or when the children were asked to help around the house, or were asked to do anything out of the ordinary, the response was a negative one. I saw many problems within this family, but the most obvious also included an inappropriate attitude being expressed by the parents toward their children. In order to get at the issue with the parents, I tried several approaches. The first being to verbally explain to the parents their attitude toward their children. The attitude was a very negative one. Commands were spoken in a "put down" language. The children were not given credit for their ability to do the chores correctly. When the chores were done the parents often criticized what had been done without ever letting the children know that they had accomplished something right. The children expressed this feeling to the parents as I presented my observations to the parents. Still the parents could not understand what was being told to them. Frank and Mary felt that this was a misperception on the children's part and on my part. Finally, after several sessions of trying to help the parents understand what part of the problem might be within their family dynamics, I asked them to give permission for the family to be videotaped. They agreed, and within two weeks we had a videotape session that included everyone in the family. As the family watched the videotape, they noticed for the first time that a lot of what they were actually saying was not being expressed in their bodily reaction to their children. The parents saw the contortions on heir own faces. They noticed their tones of voice. They saw the rigid stance they took when they communicated with their children. They noticed the anger in their eyes. In this particular family, communication patterns were very obvious and could readily be visualized through the aid of a videotape. The learning process was magnificent and the progress within the family moved rapidly after this session.

Often, as parents communicate to their children, their words do not match the reactions of their body. An example of this would be a parent trying to tell her children that she loves them when she has just spent the entire day yelling at the children to do their chores. The words, "i love you" come out of the mouth of the parent, but the look in the eye and the facial expression do not convey that message. Much of the communication that we give to those around us is nonverbal, and nonverbal communication leaves a lot of room for error, a lot of room for misperception, and for miscommunication.

Parents' attitude toward their children does affect the behavior of their children. The attitude the parents verbally and nonverbally express communicate how they regard the "personhood" of their child. If this attitude is often negative, the child, more than likely, will grow up feeling negative about himself or herself. This negative attitude takes its toll in time. On the other hand, I'm not telling parents to have a perfect attitude about their children at all times—this is next to impossible. Their overall attitude, however, needs to be accepting, and the overall messages given to the child need to be more positive than negative.

How you feel about yourself; what you believe about yourself, also affects your children. If you never really believed in yourself, if you didn't believe that you were a person of worth or value, and as a result, you had very little esteem regarding yourself, this attitude will, more than likely be conveyed to your children. Your children will begin to believe that you don't have much faith in yourself. It also may happen that you pass on this non-acceptance of yourself to non-acceptance of your children. Your children may not believe that they are persons of worth.

An interesting example of this is a lady named Joyce, who had a very critical father, a very non-accepting father.

This is a very common phenomenon within the family structure. Many families use this criticism/rejection as a means of controlling their children. As a result, in many families this negativism became entrenched within the family dynamics and caused many problems. Joyce, as an aftermath of having a critical father, spent most of her first 30-35 years being critical of others—not accepting self—being critical of what she did—being critical of her children. Joyce found herself looking for the negative in whatever she did and whatever her children did. She was patterning herself after her father; until one day, she got feedback from one of her peers at work and from some of her close friends around her, that they were tired of the way she was responding to them and to her own life. This is an unusual circumstance and does not happen very often, but Joyce was fortunate to have such open friends who were able to talk to her about her behaviors. As a result of this confrontation, Joyce made some radical changes in the way she looked at life and in her attitude, not only toward herself, but toward her children and her spouse. The change was slow but it was dramatic! The results were worth the effort of the change. Joyce realized that parents who don't feel love within themselves have a hard time giving that feeling of love to their children and that this attitude will be picked up by them. They could pick up this unspoken attitude—this unspoken inability to express feeling—this unspoken attitude that loving others is not the thing to do.

The attitude needed by a child is one of acceptance of him/her as a person. Children need to believe that they have acceptance by their parents and this acceptance is expressed not only by the words, but more importantly by the nonverbal attitude of the parents toward their children.

One of the most difficult tasks is for a parent to be open to the idea of self-exploration as to their own attitudes toward themselves and their children. It is easier to hide behind yourself than it is to look at your self openly and honestly.

Just listen to the words of a 35-year-old woman who I quoted at the beginning of this chapter. Listen to what she is saying about how the attitude of her parents' affected her. How she is now beginning to be open to looking at herself and looking at what she needs to do; what attitude she needs to take on in order for self-improvement.

"Peace of mind! I said I didn't know what that was; wrong! Peace of mind is forgiving myself for things I've done that give me an excuse to dislike me. It's accepting areas in my life I cannot change, like my dad's alcoholism. I have to learn to live without it. By that I mean, I have to stop letting it control who I am. I can now honestly say and accept that I will never get from my parents what I feel they failed to give me; that is an identity...I want to learn to say to me, 'I like you,' but instead I wait for others to say they like me, and then instead of saying, 'Yes, they're right,' I question why. Everything is not life or death! Everything is not so serious! Sure, I have times of genuine sadness, but most are self-imposed punishments for things I cannot change; for things I do not control...I do feel better now and I need to push myself into doing things about it. I'm unfortunately one of those who must learn how to have fun; let go, rather than it being a natural reaction. Natural conditioning for me is to hide, play it safe, keep my distance. What have I gotten from this approach? Pain! A lot of unnecessary, and yes, self-imposed hurt and pain. Enough! So what if you get a little hurt? You've handled hurt! That's never been a problem. Now, 'Good boy!', that's scary feeling good. That's like explaining what it feels like to walk on the moon when you've never done it. That's crap! I feel good a lot of times! I've just always dismissed it as a single event that just happened by accident and not because that's what life is—good! I don't expect never-ending feelings of bliss—I don't expect a life without disappointments, but I have a right and the obligation to myself and those I love so deeply to stop this self-hatred, guilt, and self-imposed fear. How? I guess in part by not giving in to those feelings; by allowing myself the freedom to feel good just because! No over-examined reasoning...just because!"

The young woman quoted above was stating very openly and honestly that her attitude that she had nurtured, needed to be changed. She openly admitted that she, herself, had an improper attitude and needed to work on herself. She needed to do this not only for herself, but for her child and for her husband. She, at least, was finally aware that her own attitude was hurting herself. She was aware that she was affecting her child and those other people in her life that she loved.

At the beginning of the book, I asked you to keep an open mind. I asked you to be willing to look at things without being prejudiced and that that would be a very difficult task. I am going to again ask you to look at *your attitude*; to look at how you are affecting others in your life. You may begin this by answering, to yourself, some of the following questions:

1. Do you like yourself? If not, what don't you like? Does this quality "rub off" onto your children? How will you begin to turn this dislike into a like?

2. What changes can you make to improve your attitude? What is your attitude? How do people respond to you? You may want to ask your friends about your attitude. Ask your spouse what attitude you portray to him or her and to the

children. Ask your children what attitude of yours that they would like to see you change.

3. What is your attitude and philosophy toward life? If poor, what are you going to do to change this? If good, do people *really* feel this attitude being expressed by you?

4. What gestures/motions do you use that seem most annoying to others? What do you look like to others when you are angry? Frustrated? In love?

5. If you were married to yourself, what attitude would you change?

6. If you were parenting yourself, what attitude would you change?

One last question that needs to be addressed: What if I feel my attitude is good, but no one else does? The answer is complicated but simple. It is difficult for each of us to really see, hear, and feel the reaction of ourselves to others. We often know what we intend by what we say, but often that intention is not gotten across to others. We love our children, but that message is often lost in our responses to them. We love our spouse, but our responses to him/her seems just the opposite. If we are communicating a positive attitude, we need to make sure the receiver is getting the message. The receiver may not be receptive, the sender may not be sincere, the nonverbal messages may be confusing, or the verbal messages may not be clear. It is important to remember that your intentions may be good, but for many reasons, the receiver of your message is "turned off" by his/her perception of your attitude. My message to you is *check your attitude.*

Attitude can make or break your life. Attitude can make or break a relationship. Attitude can destroy the love between you and your child.

Has the key turned in the lock and opened up a new way of dealing with yourself and your family?

THOUGHTS

- Your attitude can be misjudged by others. Ask them what they feel about your attitude, e.g., spouse, children, co-workers.

- Do not assume that because you understand your attitude, that others also understand your attitude.

- Assume nothing about the reason for another person's attitude unless you first check it out with him/her.

- Misunderstood attitudes have caused much pain in families.

- Be brave and check your attitude by asking those around you to give you feedback.

14 EXPRESSED PROBLEMS OF YOUNG PEOPLE: LISTEN

It is probably evident to you as parents that dealing with young people and their discipline problems and showing affection to them is not quite as simple as maybe you had originally thought. Human beings are very complicated. When I deal with a child, with a young adult, or with a parent, I treat each one of them as a unique piece of art. Each one has its own special colors. Each person is complete with his own identity and his own set of feelings. As I help this unique piece of art work, I look for and use his strengths to help him further himself as *that unique person*. I do not try to mold him into my way of thinking. I do not try to mold him into ways that would be contrary to his own individuality. I do, however, present alternatives that help him become more productive. It may take a jolt to his system in order to make him aware that some of his actions are destructive, either to himself or to others.

In looking at the problems of the young people, it becomes evident that the whole unique person is involved as well as the entire unique family. How that young person reacts to himself and to his family will determine the nature of the problem, if any. Past experiences have taught me that problems in a family greatly affect the well-being of the young adult. His uniqueness has been molded by those with whom he has lived most of his early life. Any dysfunction within that circle of people will definitely leave its effects on that young person. Home is a great influence on these young people as will be seen in the problem areas as expressed by them.

The following problem areas of young people are being presented in order to bring an awareness to others how troubled youth perceived the impact of their families on their lives. Most of these thoughts came from young adults between the ages of 13 and 18. All of them had received treatment for their problems either in an outpatient therapy setting, or else they were hospitalized in an adolescent treatment center.

As parents, keep this statement in mind: *Most parents have the highest intention of doing what is right for their child.* Those who don't care what happens to their child are not reading this book. Even though parents act in good faith when they deal with their child, the child does not always see this good faith or the good intention. What we do as parents, even if done in good faith, may be inappropriate. When appropriate, the actions may be misperceived by the children as being hurtful to them. In reading these following statements, try to keep an *open mind.* Try putting yourself in the shoes of the young adult.

EXPECTATIONS

One young lady was afraid to try anything new in her life as she felt that she would fail by not meeting the expectations of her dad. She realized that no matter how hard she tried, she would never please her father. She had this need, this very strong need, to please her father in order to get his conditional affection, his approval, his conditional acceptance of her. But it became too painful to try because even when she did succeed in getting approval, it was only temporary and she needed to try again. She gave up trying and found it less painful to not meet any of his expectations. It was emotionally a lot safer for her. Even today there is still a desire to seek this conditional approval.

EMPTINESS

Another young lady wanted her absent father to be present in her life. He had left when she was much younger. She did not stay close to him, in fact, she never felt close to him even when he was in her life. She states that she continues to look for someone to help her fulfill that empty emotional spot in her life. She has used sex to meet these needs, but did not find it to be very lasting. Today, she continues to seek fulfillment from other men, but refuses to let herself get close to them. She is afraid of getting emotionally hurt.

REJECTION

Many young adults and many children have stated that they are afraid of emotionally losing their parent if they stand up to them to express what they feel. For some young people it is apparent that they need to state that they hurt or feel angry or upset. They also need to be able to state that they feel very warm and close to a parent. These expressions remain unstated because permission to openly discuss these feelings within the household has not been given. This is especially true in families where there is an alcoholic. The child then directs the feelings inward or inappropriately acts out his/her feelings rather than take the risk of expressing them. I have seen this happen in many family situations, but often the parents are not aware that this emotional distancing is occurring between themselves and their children.

SELF-REJECTING

Other children and young adults state that they don't like themselves; they don't feel that they can ever succeed or ever do anything right. It became very evident that one of their parents or sometimes both of the parents were being very critical of the actions of their child. This constant criticism over the years made its mark by instilling in the young adult the belief that they were no good; that no matter what they did, they were criticized for not doing it well enough. As a result, the image of themselves became very negative and is still present today.

OVER-DEPENDENCE

It can happen that young adults become too close to the divorced parent with whom they live the majority of the time. Usually the oldest child takes on some of the roles of the absent parent and becomes, so to speak, the missing adult in the family. This can create a closeness between the child and the single parent which doesn't allow for the young adult to enjoy his youth. This does not allow the possibility of limit setting by the parent who now has a child who believes that he is equal to the parent. Sometimes the problems are brought to the young adult to solve for the single parent. These burdens, these problems become too much for these young minds to continuously handle. It is very important to keep the children after a divorce as children and not give them equal status as an adult. These young adults realized these responsibilities and power being given to them. They wanted this at first, but hated it later. They were losing the freedom of being young.

RULES TOO LATE

There are problems with parents who do not set rules until their children get older. This becomes a problem because when young, the child never learns that he has to obey, and when he gets older he does not believe that he has to follow these new rules. Parents often defend themselves by saying that their child was so good that they never needed to punish him. There are at least some minor infractions that could have been enforced that would have set the precedent for the adult setting limits early in the child's life. Curfew time, setting up a list of chores for the young adults, and use of the telephone are all examples of letting your child know that there are limits.

UNAWARENESS

Many young adults felt that it was very difficult for them to express feelings when this expression was not experienced at home. They realized after a period of time in dealing with the emotions of other young adults that they were not able to express what they felt as they had never learned how to do this. This lack of emotional output, when brought to their awareness opened new avenues of expression. Most of these young people felt more complete with their new-found ability.

PROBLEM REPETITION

In dealing with the problems of the young adult we find that often there exists the very same problem in the young adult that the parents had when they were going through their teen years. The same conflict can arise again. An example would be: A mother was suicidal about a relationship when she was a teenager; she finds that her daughter is also suicidal about a relationship she is now having with her boyfriend. It is difficult to explain why these same problems occur, especially in cases where no one knew of the parent's problem. The fact is that it does occur and parents need to be aware of what their limitations and problems were as a teenager. If these problems and limitations were not resolved, they may return again during their son's or daughter's teen years.

DIVORCE PROBLEMS

This is one of the most often mentioned problems. Divorce definitely has a negative effect on children and on teenagers. This negative effect is reduced if both parents continue to be a part of their children's lives. The breaking up of a family unit will usually take its toll. Children and young adults will need your help or other's help in dealing with divorce. Time will help heal these wounds and remove the pain.

NEED FOR LOVE

Another often expressed statement by children and young adults focuses on their need to *receive and feel acceptance from their parents*. I have yet to find a young adult who did not want his biological parents to accept him. This is a very important fact and it needs to be underscored. *Once you are the biological parents of a child you are always an important factor in his or her life.* Whether it be an effective influence or an ineffective influence, you are still a factor in their lives, so please make it effective. You can never remove yourself from being his parent. No one can take your place. It is your privilege as well as your duty to be there.

This chapter was devoted to making you a little more aware of the problems of young adults. Young children, also, are having very similar concerns. Suicidal attempts and suicidal thoughts are happening much earlier in children's lives as well as depression and anxiety. An ever-increasing problem is the use of drugs and alcohol by young children. An often not discussed issue that has serious emotional consequences is sexual and physical abuse by a parent. These are just some of the major concerns of young adults for which professional help is often needed. A high percentage of all hospitalized children and adolescents have come from a home where one or both parents are alcoholic or where one parent has been either sexually or physically abusive. The list goes on. Children do have problems. Please get them help when you become aware of their need.

THOUGHTS

- Young people do have problems and need to be heard.

- Alcoholism, physical, verbal, and sexual abuse top the list of problem concerns stemming from the family of young adults.

- There are many troubled youth who do not seek help and live in pain.

- Until young adults get the help they need, suicide rates will continue to rise.

15 EXAMPLES OF SETTING LIMITS

The need to set limits has been discussed. The results and general consensus of opinion remains firm. Limits are needed for children. Methods were then offered to you that could be used in enforcing these limits. Finally, I am going to offer you a sample of some common rules found in homes along with a selection of consequences that have been successfully used in enforcing these rules. Ages of the children will be mentioned in relation to the rules and their consequences.

Remember that these rules and consequences may not work for your family. The rules and their consequences need to be individualized for each family. Don't forget that the attitude surrounding the enforcing of the rules is as important as the rules themselves.

Here are some general rules for four to ten year old children:

Rule: There will not be any sassing toward mother or father. (This rule may need to be made clearer to the child by giving examples of their past examples of sassing.)

Consequences:

1. The child will apologize to the person he/she sassed; or 2. Apologize and spend five minutes in time out; or 3. Apologize and have the child reword to the person something more appropriate to say. (Unless the child is too young or too angry to handle this.) or 4. Other options of your own.

Rule: There will not be any hitting of your brother or sister. (The need for this rule depends on whether they get out of control when they fight each other. Parents need to avoid hitting the children if they are fighting. When parents hit the children, it only reinforces that hitting people is okay.)

Consequences:

Place in time out for five to fifteen minutes, depending on age. If both were fighting, place both in time out. Do not try to decide who was at fault if both were involved; or 2. Make them apologize to each other for hitting the other. As a result of hitting, each child also loses one hour of TV (prime time TV if you wish); or 3. Those who were fighting need to expend some of that energy more productively by doing a five to fifteen minute chore such as picking up his room or picking up his toys, etc.; or 4. Other options of your own.

Rule: Child must be in bed by 9:00 P.M. (The time will vary according to age.)

Consequences:

Child (if old enough to be aware of time) will go to bed one half hour earlier the next night for not getting to bed on time; or 2. Child will miss the usual five minute story that mom or dad tells/reads to the children before they go to sleep; or 3. For every minute the child is late getting to bed, he/she will have to go to bed that many minutes times two the next night; or 4. Other options of your own.

The following are some examples of rules and consequences for 11 to 17 year old children:

Rule: Be in by the time established for curfew. (This will vary with age and local custom of the family and the city. When a young adult is late, first check to see that they are okay and then ask why they were late. There are only a few legitimate excuses.)

Consequences:

For every minute late, the child will come in a minute times two (or times three) earlier the next comparable night. e.g., 15 minutes late on Saturday evening means coming in 30 minutes (or 45 minutes) earlier the next Saturday night; or 2. The child will be grounded for one night; or 3. The child will lose one day of telephone privileges; or 4. An option of your choice.

Rule: The child will not use the telephone after 10:00 P.M. (This time depends on the custom of the family and local circumstances.)

Consequences:

1. Loss of telephone use for one day if caught using the telephone after 10:00 P.M.; or 2. Grounding for one evening; or 3. Help mom (or dad) cook dinner and do the dishes the next evening (if this isn't already part of his chores.); or 4. An option of your choosing.

Rule: There will be no leaving the house after bed time. (Sneaking out can be very serious depending on what is done by the child while he or she is out of the house. If stealing, using or selling drugs, or other illegal actions are occurring, then these consequences may not be enough. Counseling and/or involvement of the juvenile office may be necessary.)

Consequences:

1. If caught, the child will be grounded for the weekend; or 2. If sneaking out continues to occur, the child will come home right after school until at least two weeks go by without any sneaking out; or 3. A change in bedrooms to keep the child from sneaking out; or 4. An option of your choice.

Rule: Grades must be kept to at least a "C". (This rule is only good if the child is capable of *a t least* "C" work or better. To some children, a "C" is equal to an "A+". Check with the school as your child's potential to get a "C".)

Consequences:

A one to one-and-a-half hour study time at home will be set up on Sunday through Thursday nights. During this time there is no television, loud music, or telephone use. A parent can check on the grades three weeks after the study time was enforced to see if the grades have risen to at least a "C" or "C-." If so, the study time then again becomes voluntary. I do not require higher than a "C" as I consider the higher grades to be part of the child's personal motivation to raise them above a "C."

Overall, be creative in setting the consequences for your limits. As for the limits themselves, be to the point. Make them clear and understandable. Don't say, "Be home shortly after the show," unless you have a self-restricting and reasonable young adult. State that you would like him/her home no later than 30 minutes after the show is over. Be fair with the limits. Most limit setting serves a purpose.

The above examples were given to help you understand some of the types of limits and their consequences that are used by other families. The more difficult child/young adult will not respond to the typical rules. These children/young adults may need special help, such as counseling. The whole family may benefit from some forms of counseling.

When you have tried everything, but still do not seem to be making any headway, then it is time to seek professional help.

THOUGHTS

- Limits are necessary.

- Rules vary from family to family, just as do consequences.

- When in doubt about a rule or a consequence, ask the opinion of other parents.

- You can be too strict as well as too lenient. Both can negatively affect the child.

- There is a time when professional help may be necessary.

16 WHAT ARE YOU REALLY TRYING TO SAY WHEN . . .

Have you really looked at the messages you send to your children? What hidden messages are included in the transmission to the child? What nonverbal signals tag along with the verbal message? Children and young adults perceive messages from their own world which may be different from yours. Therefore, what you send may not be received as you intended.

The following messages from adults to children are a challenge to adults to take a look at their messages.

What are you really trying to say when. . .

. . .you hit your kids as a punishment for fighting with each other and then say, "You and your brother should not hit each other."?

. . .you tell your child not to smoke as it is bad for his health, yet you do not try to quit smoking yourself?

. . .you criticize your child day in and day out for every detail he does wrong, but expect him to feel good about himself?

. . .you cannot show your children that you love them by hugging them or telling them, yet expect them to know that you love them?

. . .You curse at people, but slap your child when he/she curses? The parents are the model for their child.

. . .you expect your child not to lie, but she hears you tell your boss you are sick when you are really planning to go out of town on a shopping trip?

. . .you expect your children never to disagree with you when in fact they hear you constantly fighting with your spouse, putting down your boss's rules, or showing disrespect to your own parents?

. . .you expect your child to be happy when you haven't been happy in years?

. . .you expect your child to always pick up after himself when you consistently leave a trail of litter behind you?

. . .you expect your child/young adult to not to be tempted to drink alcoholic beverages when in fact the first thing you reach for at night is a can of beer to take the "edge" off of your hard day?

. . .you yell at your child and say he/she is dumb, stupid, and worthless, yet you want him/her to achieve great things for himself/herself?

. . .you emotionally reject your child through verbal put downs or through physical distancing?

What is the message the country gives to its children when. . .

. . .violence is used to settle disputes?

. . .immediate gratification of needs is the aim of most commercials?

. . .attainment of money becomes the highest priority in a nation?

. . .when the value of learning is superseded by the value of what you can monetarily get out of it?

. . .we have so much crime that we can't trust those we do not know and suspiciousness becomes the general attitude?

. . .drugs are used for immediate gratification of needs without regard for personal well-being?

. . .the product sold is more important than the effect the product has on the person who buys it?

. . .material possessions are often touted as the means to a joy-filled life?

Fortunately it is not all that bleak. There are people in the country and families that do extol qualities and values that help the nation and its members live a meaningful existence! However, that is not good enough. Too many harmful values and attitudes reach our children. The nation and its adults must begin to realize that their actions as individuals and as a collective group do influence the children around them. What happens in the home influences the *heartbeat* of the nation. What is said and what is done by example will effect those emotionally close to us and those living around us. Look inward and realize the power of your actions and words. Speak and act only in the way that you would like to be *treated*. The power for good is within you, but so can the power to hurt or destroy be born from you.

THOUGHTS

- Your words and actions affect more people's lives than you are aware.

- Your words and actions as a parent can affect generations of your offspring.

- Your role in the country as a citizen and worker influences the values that are seen and felt by your children.

- The values of the nation influence the children that it governs.

- Whenever a person cheats, steals, lies, becomes violent, hates, rejects, these actions continue their effect in the lives of those around that person.

- Loving actions and words go a long way.

17 ARE PROBLEMS ONLY ALL EMOTIONAL?

"I have tried everything I know with my child, yet nothing seems to be changing. Where do I turn next? I don't understand what is happening." These are the words of many parents who have become frustrated with the lack of change in their child's reaction to life and family. They have read books and sought out answers, but to no avail. They did not check out, however, if there could have been some physical causes of their child's behavior. Because he/she was healthy, they assumed that there was nothing wrong physically.

Not all behaviors of a child have a physical cause just as not all behaviors of a child are exclusively psychological in nature. The mind and the body work together. Both areas need to be checked out. Psychiatrists, physicians, psychologists, counselors, social workers, and ministers all need to work together in understanding the particular problem of this particular child. The battle between psychologists and psychiatrists needs to stop. Joining knowledge with personal experiences needs to occur for the benefit of those seeking services.

There are too many areas to detail in this book which could involve medical and psychological overlap. This overlap is questioned by many as non-existent. Others recognize the overlap as a real situation. Depression is an excellent example. Is there a biochemical predisposition of depression? Does a person's life circumstances alone cause depression? Are anti-depressants effective in relieving depression? Can allergies or certain other physical illnesses cause depression? Do changes in seasons cause depression?

The answer to what causes depression is non-specific and depends on the individual situation. All of the above alternatives do have the possibility of affecting depression, each in its own way. The conclusion I am reaching states that emotional concerns can have roots in both the physical and psychological (environmental) world. Neither is mutually exclusive of each other.

Treatment of emotional problems can also be a combination of medical and psychological (non-medical) methods. (Please realize I have simplified the differences in treatment to medical and psychological, which is not an accurate separation of the choices available.) The evidence increases as to the effectiveness of psychotherapy. Chemical treatment of certain types of emotional problems has also attained great support for its effectiveness. Many practitioners use a combination of both approaches, again depending on the nature of the problem.

A good practitioner/psychotherapist will help assess (or refer for assessment if the problem is out of his/her expertise) the problem and the best approach to use in the situation presented to him/her. Being willing to recognize the abilities of other professionals in the same and other related fields is of significant importance. The openness to alternative solutions is what needs to be considered. A good practitioner will consider all possible alternatives to the solution of the problem and inform their client of the choices available.

What does all of this have to do with being an effective parent? As an effective parent you need to be aware of the choices available to you as a treatment approach for you and your family members. You also need to be aware that a particular emotional problem can have a physiological root base. Rule out all that you can in seeking the origins of a problem.

Will this information help you add to your own knowledge needed to resolve the problems presented to you?

THOUGHTS

- The emotions and body work together to form the person along with the intellectual and spiritual realms.

- Emotional problems can have a physiological component.

- A good practitioner/psychologist will be aware of the interactions of the medical and emotional worlds on a person's problem.

- Solutions to a problem can involve the cooperation of practitioners in many fields. Neither the emotions nor the body live in isolation of each other.

18 PARENTS IN CONFLICT WITH PARENTS

As I continue to work with families and couples, I am surprised at the conflict and unresolved issues that surface in adults regarding their parenting as a child. Many of these unresolved and still present conflicts carry down to conflicts within their immediate family. This was never more evident than the time when four generations of one family brought to me the youngest member who was starting to exhibit the same problem as experienced by the three previous generations. It was unusual that no one had a clue as to the nature of that family problem.

An example of a generational conflict would be parents who have exceedingly high expectations for their children. So high are these expectations that often the children give up trying to meet them. While the children are still aspiring to please, the parents may also be caught in their own web of continuing to live up to what they feel their parents want them to do. Sometimes this becomes a never ending cycle of living up to other's unattainable wishes! This web can entangle generation after generation unless resolved.

For many families, the problem or conflict is never recognized. The problem is handled the way it always has been with the solution being the same. Once a solution is learned, it is difficult to change it. Unfortunately, many solutions are not effective and cause family discord. Being open to new solutions is a gift people need.

Other examples of unresolved family conflicts abound in my private practice. Recently a thirty-five year old mother of five children brought me her daughter who at age fourteen was rebelling and refusing to do what her mom wished. At the same time this was happening the mother, Jennifer, was divorcing her husband, the girl's father. The daughter was fighting the divorce as well as mom's extremely high expectations of her. The mother, not aware of her impact on her daughter, continued her high demands thinking she was being the perfect mother.

Jennifer then come alone into therapy with her own multiple concerns and began the unfolding of her feelings. The emotions flowed as she described her life and how unhappy she was not only now but in her childhood. She felt like she could never please anyone. When she did something that displeased her parents, her husband or her children, she felt guilty. No matter how hard she tried, she always ended up not meeting their expectations. To her, she had failed in their eyes. She felt she was not loved because to displease by failing to meet up to a standard meant emotional rejection. Jennifer felt this rejection from her parents. Eventually she felt this about her husband and finally by her children. The mother lived to please others. She never felt any pleasure in doing something for herself. She lived only to try and meet *all* the expectations that others placed on her.

After several sessions of exploring her feelings which were buried deep within her, Jennifer began to realize that she was still trying to please her mother and father in all that she did. They would not accept her for divorcing. They felt she wasn't handling her children appropriately. Jennifer decided she had to fight back by rejecting them. She was not aware that she was also placing these same demands on her daughter.

This is only one example of a conflict that is passed down from one family to the next generation. The inability to realize how you affect your children is so real and so common. Neither generation saw what was happening within their own immediate family. Their eyes were blinded, their ears shut by their own belief system.

Today as a therapist, I often work with parents and their parents as they deal with old issues that are still in effect years after the children leave home. Such issues involve emotional abuse, inability to express feelings, inability to see another viewpoint, inability to set definite limits or the inability to show love that can actually be felt by someone else in the family.

As a therapist, I feel the next area in psychology to receive focus is that of adults as the children dealing with their parents on issues that remain unresolved. It will probably be the adult children who initiate this process. This is so important if any progress is to be made in dealing with today's children. It will take courage to face the old issues but the results of resolving these issues have proven to be very rewarding. Parents dealing with parents in an effective manner will generate more effective parenting with the next generation.

One of the most moving experiences that I encounter in therapy involves an adult, who is the child, finally believing that they are loved by their parents. (I also enjoy this with children.) Even though most parents feel they have shown love to their children, this is often not perceived as such. These children grow into adults not feeling loved. They often fear they will never be loved, yet they can't seem to challenge this belief by talking these issues out with their parents. This *needless distance* goes on for years. Getting adults (child) to openly deal with the unspoken feelings of the past with their older parents is resisted. The fears of childhood are still present in the adult. They may be masked by anger or "I don't need their love" expressions but they are there. Once the adult, who is the child, realizes that they can talk to their parents about past issues without the fear of rejection, it becomes possible to arrange a meeting to discuss these issues.

Before this meeting begins, it is necessary for a therapist or an intermediary to talk to the adult parents about what is going to take place. Explain the purpose and intent of the meeting and how their children have questions about how past happenings were perceived and then felt. This is not a time where people are put down but rather it is a time of clarification of feelings that surround certain past events. I find parents most willing to attend a meeting or a session where clarification takes place. Most parents have always had good intentions with regards to their children but "mess up" in their attempts to carry these out.

In the process of talking openly, both generations need to clearly and effectively express their love for each other until it is acknowledged as felt by the others. Once this love is believed and felt, issues of conflict are easier to discuss and resolve. Such a beautiful experience. It adds years to my life to see this process unfold. Try it. You will like it. Generally, there is no reason for parents to remain in conflict with their own parents. It only creates problems for future generations.

THOUGHTS

- Unresolved conflicts with our parents can affect how we parent our own children.

- The love from a parent needs to be felt.

- Clearing up troublesome issues from the past is not as difficult as it seems.

- Understanding our parents *real intentions* may be pleasantly surprising.

- Be brave and as adults begin a more open dialogue of thoughts and feelings with your parents.

19 HOW TO TALK TO YOUR CHILDREN

Quietly, calmly, and with a genuine concern you begin to discuss your son's disagreement with your rule of 11:30 curfew. He retorts, "All the other parents let their kids stay out until at least 1:00. I feel so stupid coming in so early. You are dumb parents. I would be better off in prison." As his voice rises and negative comments continue, you begin to feel your blood pressure rise, your body tense, and your voice take on an angry pitch. Suddenly the words come forth from your mouth to your son, "All you do is fight our rules, complain about the food we eat, and refuse to do anything we ask. Why don't you go live somewhere else?" At that point your son turns around and walks out the door.

It is precisely at these moments when a parent needs to know how to communicate with his or her children. How do you talk to an angry son who doesn't want to listen? What are some general ways to get children to listen?

There are several purposes in communicating with your children. For the sake of simplicity, I divide these purposes into two general tasks. The first task is to enforce the limits that have been set as house rules. The second task is to openly talk to a son or daughter with the sole purpose being to understand his or her feelings, thoughts, and values regarding self and family. For the first type of communication, the parent has the upper hand. The result of the communication will be the enforcement of a rule or value!

"Mom, I want to go to a concert in _____ with my boyfriend, John and our friends. We will have to be gone all night, but John has a friend who will put us up for the night at his place."

"Judy, as your mother, you know I can't approve of this. You are only 14. I feel it is not okay for you to be gone all night with your boyfriend, especially since John's friend is only 17 and living on his own. Under other circumstances, I might have considered it."

As a parent you need to communicate well enough to know the facts presented to you. The final decision, however, is not based on good communication, but on the family values and rules.

Rules need to be discussed and parents need to be open to new thoughts on the matter. But as your child grows up, parental values need to be made clear. Listening to you child's views is very important. Trying to see where they stand; trying to put yourself in their footsteps can be helpful in rule decision making. Until they are on their own, the house rules belong to the parents' domain (as long as the parents make appropriate rules and treat their child with dignity and respect).

The other type of communication involves less of a parenting role and more of an unbiased listener. For example, your daughter isn't sure how she feels about John, her boyfriend. She wants to tell you that she has thought about dating others but doesn't know if she can handle this. She comes to you to have someone to listen to her views.

As a listener, you need to practice your established communication skills. You will include some of the following in an attempt to hear what your daughter is saying:

1. Let her know you hear what she is saying by repeating or rephrasing what you hear her telling you. "Judy, if I hear you correctly, you can't decide if you can emotionally handle dating another boy while going with John?"

   "Yeah, mom. I feel it may confuse me as to my feelings for John. But I would still like to give it a try, as John and I have our differences."

2. When you are trying to listen, do not destroy the conversation by nagging, putting the child/young adult down, criticizing, moralizing, giving a lecture, or other approaches that steer the conversation away from the speaker.

   "Judy, John is such a klutz. You need to get another boyfriend. It's about time you got some sense in that thick skull of yours." This latter communication is a "stopper". For all practical purposes the conversation stops with the last statement.

3. You need to realize that your child has feelings also. Try to find out what they are. Do not expect them to be the same as yours. He/she is a unique being in his/her own right.

4. Reflect back a child's feeling to make a check as to whether you understood them.

   "Judy, if I hear you correctly, you are feeling that..."

5. Keep good eye contact with the child/young adult. Also, externally show that you are interested in what is being said.

6. Try to ask questions rather than answer them, unless asked to do so.

7. Realize that the purpose of this communication is to understand the feelings and thinking of your child, not to prove your point or use your "muscle" as a parent. There is a time and a place for those other types of communication.

There is so much more to communication than what I have stated. There are many good books and tapes on how to communicate. My purpose in this chapter was to have you look at your communication with your child. Does it need more work? Do you need to listen more often? Can you listen without always answering with a parental guideline? Do you know when to listen and offer advice and when to enforce a rule?

In general, remember that your children/young adults like to be listened to and respected as beings in their own right. Children like to know that their feelings are being noticed; that mom and dad do understand (not necessarily agree) how they can hurt, feel sad, be angry at the world.

If you have listened well to your children/young adults, you will know what to say to them as you respond to them. As they continue to grow and develop their feelings and their minds, you, as a parent, begin to offer fewer answers, and instead help the children/young adults find their own appropriate answers. This process begins early when you offer your children a choice of behavioral responses ("Do you want to go to bed now, or go to bed earlier tomorrow night?").

Communication is vital in a family. Treat your child like you would like to be treated. Talk to your child like you want to be talked to. Respect your child like you want to be respected. Continue to challenge yourself to listen. *Key* in on the messages being sent to you by your child.

THOUGHTS

- Poor communication in a family can result in a family breakdown.

- Good communication must involve good listeners. The parents must be good listeners to model this behavior for their children.

- Enforcing rules, enforcing a family standard of living, being firm in your beliefs is just one kind of communication. However, it can easily turn into a one-sided conversation.

- Listening to your child means letting him/her express what is going on inside his/her head and heart (feelings) without your needing (at this time) to stand in judgment over these thoughts and feelings.

- Learn to talk without always giving an answer or standing in judgment of what is being said.

- Listen to yourself when you talk. How does it sound?

20 ALCOHOL AND DRUGS

What a problem for the country and the world. So much is being written and so many plans being proposed to remedy this body and mind destroying habit. I can add very little to the information presented. I can, however, offer a challenge to parents and to those who influence the young.

The challenge involves establishing a value and attitude. The value to be promulgated is that alcohol and illicit drugs have very little importance in themselves when it comes to recreational use. The less we value these illicit drugs and alcohol, the fewer problems we will see in those around us. Many killing accidents, many illnesses, and much crime is a direct result of use of these substances. If we wish to see a continued rise in people dying on the highways, continued physical illnesses, and a rise in crime, we will continue to believe in the importance of these chemical substances. To reduce the value of these substances in our lives and in society will proportionately reduce their negative effects on the same. The choice is ours as individuals and as parents. Each one of us has to decide where these chemical substances rank in our lives (if at all).

Next, as a society, and more importantly, as a family, we must determine the attitudes that we perpetuate regarding alcohol and drug use in general. When down, when dissatisfied, when in moderate pain, do we turn to a quick fix in the form of alcohol and/or drugs? Are not many of us reaching for a pill at the first sign of discomfort? What message does this give to our young people? Do we need to consider the attitude of trying to work out our discomforts, at times, without the aid of pills or alcohol? What about the attitude of having to have alcohol/drugs to relax or to have a good time? What about the attitude of quickly getting into another mood by any artificial means? Finally, what about the attitude that we must rely on something artificial to make us happy?

The attitude within a family regarding drugs and alcohol can be a major deterrent in a child's using drugs and alcohol inappropriately. (Excluding the potential influence of the disease concept regarding alcohol and certain illicit drugs.) The family's more general attitude about using substances or pills to make one happy is also important. The family is a key to the values and attitudes with which a child forms his own opinions on alcohol and drug use. Our society which is made up of families can then begin its own change. This is a monumental task, but all other approaches seem only to put out fires. The value of drugs for happiness and pleasure must decrease or face the consequences, many of which we have already seen and fear.

THOUGHTS

- There are many reasons why drugs have taken over the control of the lives of many young people.

- An important remedy to reduce the influence of drugs on our children involves the increased positive influence of appropriate family values and attitudes.

- The importance of drugs to have fun must be replaced with some other positive experiences.

- Drugs can be the downfall of a nation. Do we care enough to speak out?

21 WHEN DO YOU TURN FOR EXPERT HELP?

Knowing when to ask for help with your child is not an easy task. No one has all the answers to the questions about children and their behavior. It is very difficult for a parent to be able to look objectively at their situations with their own children. It is so much easier to see what other people are doing wrong than it is to see our own inconsistencies and inappropriate responses. I encourage parents to ask for help when they have questions about their children. There is never a question that is too simple to ask. I use these guidelines to help parents determine when they need to turn to an expert for advice:

1. When your children tell you what to do and seem to be taking control of running the family.

2. When your children do not seem to listen to you when you are talking to them. This would include children making fun of what you say, turning away from you when you talk to them, and acting in a defiant manner.

3. When you disagree, as parents, about your next step in dealing with your children and can't seem to resolve these differences of opinions. Parents need to unite in their efforts in dealing with their children. Constant fighting over the approach to use with your children can cause a lot of turmoil within the family.

4. When your children seem to rebel against your methods of discipline. I would then suggest looking at alternative methods or else examining your present methods. Something is lacking if children

consistently rebel against your attempts to deal with their behaviors.

5. When you wish to seek alternative suggestions from an expert because you feel your parenting methods are ineffective. Talking over how you are handling your children may be very rewarding to you. You at least get a chance to get the opinion of someone who deals with children about your effectiveness in handling parent-child problems.

6. When other people begin to tell you that your children are a problem and you are not aware of this. You may wish to have someone help you get to the bottom of the issue.

Remember that a second opinion from someone who has credentials in dealing with children can be a very rewarding experience. The information obtained from talking to this expert does not have to be followed if you disagree with the approach. However, a good child specialist will take into consideration your style and your needs in dealing with your children. Many ways are appropriate in dealing with children. One method is not necessarily better than another if it does not fit your style of working with children. When you seek advice from an expert, keep an open mind to new ideas. It is very easy to say, "I have never tried this method; therefore, it is not good." Give new ideas and new methods a fair chance.

Below are some warning signals with regard to children's behaviors that might indicate that you may need to seek help with your child. This list is not all-inclusive, but covers many important facets of inappropriate and unhealthy behaviors of children.

1. When your child drastically changes his style of behaving. This is a sign that something is going

on with that child that needs attention. An example would be a child who is usually very outgoing and suddenly becomes very quiet and withdrawn. Any drastic change in behavior that lasts for more than a week or two should be a warning signal to parents that something important is going on with that child.

2. When your child's school grades take a sudden downward change. A student who goes from an "A"-"B" student to a "D"-"F" student in a short period of time is probably undergoing some type of stress. Grades can be an indicator of change within a child. All change does not necessarily have to be bad. I am asking you to check into why these changes are occurring and not to overlook their importance.

3. When your child becomes extremely aggressive and the aggressiveness cannot be handled with the typical discipline methods. Parents who cannot control the physical acting out of their children need to get help from an expert.

4. When your child becomes very withdrawn. A child who is so withdrawn that his or her interactions with others are extremely limited, needs further attention and evaluation. Extreme shyness can cause a lot of difficulty for a child later on if the child does not learn how to interact with others. A shy person can be very unhappy. Shy or withdrawn children are often overlooked as far as needing help because they do not cause a problem to people. This doesn't mean that they don't hurt inside.

5. When your child is unable to stay with one activity for at least five or ten minutes. These children are going to present a problem to themselves and to their parents in the future. These children are close to being too active to handle school work or tasks that require a lot of attention. Hyperactivity is an over-used term, and the actual causes for hyperactivity are varied. A child who is so active that he cannot sit still or cannot attend to activities for any length of time needs to be evaluated by an appropriate professional. A child who cannot pay attention to anything and who is easily distracted can have problems with behavior as well as problems in his or her attempts to learn.

6. When your child refuses to obey any adult authority figure. These children are typically in opposition to anything that is said by any adult.

7. When you are concerned that your child is unusually sad or feel that your child is acting in ways that are not typical for children. I would have that child evaluated, not only physically, but also psychologically.

8. When your child worries excessively about events in the future, he may be overanxious and need some counseling. It will become very obvious to you if your child worries too much. This will be a daily activity and you will see the child be afraid to attend to most things because of some fear or some worry that he will get hurt or that something will happen to other people. The child will do almost nothing because of the tendency to worry. This child, of course, needs help.

9. When your child steals from others, constantly lies, or constantly beats up on other children. An evaluation is needed to find the cause of these behaviors.

There is no way possible to mention all the behaviors that are warning signs to parents that a child might be in need of help. A general rule that I find very helpful is to compare the behavior of a child with a large percentage of other children. If I find this behavior unusual or inappropriate, I would then use that as a sign that something may be not right. As a parent, I would at least ask a professional about the behaviors of this child. Another general rule to follow is that if a child seems particularly unhappy or out of sorts with himself, it might be the time to check with someone regarding that child. Just like adults, children are unpredictable and there is no way to determine what is going on with the child unless the child volunteers that information to someone else. I do not like to compare one child with another, but there are certain very obvious behaviors that need to be attended to should they occur. These behaviors will stick out in a crowd of other children. They will become very obvious and should be dealt with before they become a bigger problem.

There are many sources that people can turn to for help with their children. There are many social service agencies available in communities. There are many private individuals who do counseling with children and families. Mental health centers seem to be one of the most common sources for people to turn to when children need help. Another source of help that is often overlooked are high school counselors and elementary counselors within a school system. Many times these counselors are able to detect when a child is having a problem and can refer parents to the proper agencies for help. These school counselors are very well-trained to provide counseling or will refer the child elsewhere should more intensive therapy be needed. I would encourage parents to use the services of school counselors when they are available.

At any time you receive help for your child, make sure the person has the proper credentials and training needed to deal with children. Usually a masters degree in some human service field is a minimal degree. Eventually all licensed psychologists will have a doctorate degree. *Training and experience are important.* There are people with training and qualifications that are varied and do not follow the typical pattern, but who still might be effective counselors. The most important quality is that you, as the parent, are satisfied with that person's training and experience. Typically, as you ask around the community, people will know those professionals who are effective in dealing with children and adults. Do not be afraid to ask the people to give you references before you seek help from them. I would encourage you to talk to professionals about your child as I feel you and your family will benefit from that experience.

THOUGHTS

- When you are having trouble dealing with your child, do not be afraid to ask for help.

- Be aware of the signs of a problem within a child.

- Any extreme change in behavior that persists more than several days should be a sign that something could be wrong.

- Look for help from a professional with training and experience.

- Psychotherapy/counseling should be considered as common as going to a doctor for physical problems.

22 "THE OTHER"

The pendulum must swing. The time has come for many to turn their attention to the feelings and needs of other people in their lives. Lately, the self has been of utmost importance.

In the past the self needed to be discovered/rediscovered. People got lost in other people to the exclusion of any personal self-worth. The self suffered at the hands of the other who exploited him. The self needed to emerge in order to survive and grow as a being of worth and a being of importance. Individuals began to arise, to achieve, and to become persons in their own right. A very wonderful feeling.

Like any turn around, the self in many cases did not know where to stop in its quest for survival and well-being. As the self began to feel good, it extended this feeling into all aspects of its life. The self in some instances took over in work, play, at home, and in the marriage. The self found its happiness in the self, consequently, the belief that there is no one more important than the self.

As time passed the self began to realize that taking care of itself was important, but something was missing. It didn't like to admit it, but the self was lonely. It felt greedy, self-worshiping, and unfulfilled. The self was forgetting that it existed in a big world full of other "selves" that were also becoming self-worshiping. This was a sad commentary on a good beginning—a beginning that gave the self some existence.

The self began to realize that it needed to recognize the existence of the "other". The other was the person who lived with the self, the person who was the son or daughter of the self, the person who was the co-worker of the self, the person who was the neighbor of the self.

The other had been forgotten while the self grew. The other had taken a back seat, while the self began to forget that the other even existed.

Such a sad story. The other is often forgotten today. The self often thrives and grows, finding happiness in its own existence. Yet I keep hearing that the self is lonely, that the self needs a companion. The other hears this need of the self and tries to reach out but keeps hearing from the self a rejection as the self cannot seem to open up to the other. The self retreats in loneliness.

A new day will begin when the self discovers the other. When the self sees itself in the other, when the self sees itself in its children, co-workers, spouse, and neighbors. That will be the day of all days, when the self and the other join forces to become one. A new trend should be in the making. A new understanding would be developing between the self and the other. Such an understanding can produce warmth, joy, and peace.

THOUGHTS

- The other needs to be considered.

- The self needs to recognize the other.

- The self may have over-extended its boundaries.

- Our children need to be more aware of the other.

- Harmony between the self and other can bring great things.

23 WHERE DO I GO FROM HERE?

As a parent you have already begun a journey of great significance. You have taken on a mission to continue your life's existence into many generations. You are continuing your influence into generations to come. You have decided to be the life-support, emotional support, and spiritual support for a very small and dependent human being. This support continues throughout the lifetime of your child. Such a worthy and beautiful task to undertake.

Your intentions as a parent are good. For the few of you that don't have good intentions for your role as a parent, change and begin this immediately with help from others. For the rest, as parents you want to do the best you can with what knowledge you have. Therein lies our goal. Acquire more knowledge, be open to change, and continue giving our love to our children. In so doing, you have accomplished the greatest task known to man. A task that is greater than achieving financial wealth, a task greater than accomplishing physical feats. There is no greater task than being a parent and you are worthy of the task.

Take a little trip with me--you are in a strange world of people called Andorkums. Like you, they are looking for answers to questions of importance to them. These people begin the journey of seeking knowledge in all matters. You follow along. The journey takes you into dark places that seem mysterious and foreign. You continue forth with great anticipation of things to come. The intensity builds. All in the group find little clues that spur them on to find greater knowledge. Soon people begin to split off and take separate trails. There were over 100 in your group, now you are down to ten people. Yet with these ten people, you feel comfortable as you progress in your journey. Still searching for knowledge and answers, you look everywhere. Slowly, one by one, the people who were with you take different paths. The group of ten is now down to you alone. All of your fellow travelers have left you in pursuit of their own knowledge.

Suddenly you come across a beautiful valley where contentment overcomes you. In this valley is a beautiful lake that draws you toward it. Upon reaching the lake you look down and see a face of a person who is smiling up at you. You are startled, not knowing if this person is a friendly Andorkum or not. The person tells you not to be afraid, to quietly sit down and take in the knowledge of the lake. Instantly you feel calm, relaxed, and open to the wisdom of the lake. Suddenly, a sense of well-being overcomes you. The person who was smiling at you begins to tell you things that astonish you; knowledge seems so easy at this moment. Much of importance is spoken. You are feeling so good, so delighted at your discovery of this friendly valley, friendly lake, and friendly person talking to you.

All of a sudden, the friendly face begins to fade from beneath your gaze. You panic. You can't lose this person with all this knowledge. "Come back!," you cry, "I don't even know your name." A fading voice says with a smile, as it disappears from the lake, "My name is Uoy!" Suddenly, a realization hits you. Your search is over.

What is the key to being a good parent? The answer is not only contained within the book, but within you. As you read the book, there should have been times when you realized an insight that could have been the answer for you. This answer will differ from person to person. By keeping an open mind and heart you will have found many *keys*. But the most important key surrounds you.

Over the years of working with families I often hear from the children the statement that they were not sure that their parents really loved them. They questioned whether their parents were glad to be parents. It seemed to them that they were in the way or that they couldn't please their parents or that their feelings were not important. Why were they born? Why was the attitude in the house so negative? Why were parents so difficult to understand?

The bottom line concern of many of these children/ young adults was *their perception* of not feeling a genuine interest and love from the parents. It was *their perception* that the feeling of acceptance was often not there. They were loved only if they. . . .

The key in my opinion to the *foundation* of a potentially excellent family lies in the correct perception between parents and their children of the love that is felt between them. The misperceptions of not being loved abound but are often not talked about. Because love is expressed does not mean it is felt. Parents are loving and have good intentions but these feelings are often not understood by children. This act of understanding can undermine and destroy a family. Without this understanding of love the family potentially will fail. Without a foundation, the house will crumble. Do your children really *feel* they are loved? Does your family possess this foundation?

Everyone has the ability to love but none is more important than the love children know and feel from their parents. Are your children blessed by your presenting them with the key to their well being?

The beginning.

THOUGHTS

- May you believe in what is good and valuable.

- May you believe in the power of a family.

- May you love those close to you without reservation.

- May you pass the key on to your children.

OTHER FINE BOOKS FROM R&E ! ! !

THE RECREATION OF A NATION THROUGH REAL PARENTING by Michael J. Mayer, Ed.D.. There is a key to parenting. You already have this key within you, but without understanding, you will never find it.

This book will help you discover the beauty and majesty within you that will enable you to perform the most important task of ALL—raising your children. As the author says, "Parenting has implications that reach the soul of a child and the heart of a nation."

According to psychologist Michael J. Mayer, all you need to find the key to raising your children is an open heart and an open mind. You need to take what you already know about parenting, and adjust it slightly to make it more effective, life-enhancing and loving.

$9.95   ISBN 0-88247-929-6
Soft Cover   Order #929-6

TAKING CHARGE: A PARENT AND TEACHER GUIDE TO LOVING DISCIPLINE by Jo Anne Nordling. At last, here is a book that shows both parents and teachers everything they need to know to discipline children effectively and fairly.

This easy-to-understand action guide will show you how to handle the most critical disciplinary issues in teaching and raising children.

$11.95   ISBN 0-88247-906-7
Trade Paper   Order #906-7

THE GOAL BOOK: Your Simple Power Guide to Reach any Goal & Get What You Want by James Hall. Would you like to be able to turn your dreams into realities? You can if you have concrete goals. This book is based upon a unique goal achievement technique developed by a high school teacher and career counselor in California's Silicon Valley. "Action Conditioning Technology" (ACT) will help you convert your dreams and wishful fantasies into obtainable goals. With this new achievement technology, you will be able to decide exactly what you want, what steps you need to take and when you will reach your objective.

$6.95   LC 91-50675   ISBN 0-88247-892-3
Trade Paper   6 x 9   Order #892-3

CREATIVE COMMUNICATION: How to Develop and Apply your Skills to Communicate Persuasively, Professionally and Productively by Victor Annigian. Our schools teach reading and writing, but they don't teach us how to communicate effectively. This breakthrough book will teach you the art and science of understanding others and of being understood. Filled with practical information that you can use immediately and will help you in both your business and personal relationships.

$14.95   Soft Cover   ISBN 0-88247-932-6   Order #932-6
$19.95   Hard Cover   ISBN 0-88247-933-4   Order #933-4